ALLOTTED TIME

ALLOTTED TIME
TWELVE MONTHS, TWO BLOKES, ONE SHED, NO IDEA

ROBIN SHELTON

Sidgwick & Jackson

First published 2006 by Sidgwick & Jackson
an imprint of Pan Macmillan Ltd
Pan Macmillan, 20 New Wharf Road, London N1 9RR
Basingstoke and Oxford
Associated companies throughout the world
www.panmacmillan.com

ISBN-13: 978-0-283-07032-7
ISBN-10: 0-283-07032-3

1 3 5 7 9 8 6 4 2

A CIP catalogue record for this book is available from
the British Library.

Typeset by SetSystems Ltd, Saffron Walden, Essex
Printed and bound in Great Britain by
Mackays of Chatham plc, Chatham, Kent

To my sister, and her two
remarkable nephews

'Green fingers are the extension of a verdant heart'

Russell Page, *The Education of a Gardener*

Contents

Contents

Acknowledgements

I would like to thank the following people for the following reasons: I owe all of them a huge debt of gratitude and, in many instances, a good deal of cash. They are, in chronological order, as listed below.

My mother, Elizabeth Shelton, for being right far more often than I ever give her credit for and for saying 'I told you so' far less often than many other parents would have done. My late father, for teaching me the single most important and universal philosophy I have ever learned. My sister, Jacqueline Mulvaney, whose consistent presence and importance in my life is by no means reflected in this book, for always saying 'I told you so' when I really need it saying to me, for keeping me on track in all ways, always, and for consistently reminding me that I am indeed a Womble. My brother-in-law, Jonathan Mulvaney, for stepping into two breaches, for supplying me with far more beer than I could ever replace and for teaching me all I will ever need to know about a gamut of topics I never even realized I didn't know about.

I owe my most trusted and long-standing friend, who is not also family, Jeremy O'Kill, an enormous amount for his support and understanding and for being the

ACKNOWLEDGEMENTS

most striking example of true individuality it will ever
be my privilege to know. It is a pleasure to thank and
send all my love to my two cherished sons, Gabriel and
Dylan Shelton, for their amazing maturity in understanding how important this project has been to me,
and for allowing me to pursue it. I would like to record
my highest admiration for my great friend and the only
picture framer I know who does not cut corners, Simon
Quinn, for frequently making me feel slipshod, uninfor-
med and ineloquent, and for demonstrating that frisbee
throwing is truly an art form.

The allotment, and therefore this book, would simply
not have happened were it not for my neighbour and
indispensable friend Stevie Newcombe – therefore half
the credit (or blame) rests squarely with him. People of
his calibre do not cross our paths often. I have learned
that when they do it is as well to be as rude as is
humanly possible to them. They seem to like it. If his
wife, Lizzie, who also does not get mentioned nearly as
often as she might in this text, had not been around to
tell Stevie which end of the fork to hold when I was
away, all hell would have broken loose. She is more
than 'Steve's wife' to me, and I count myself highly
fortunate to also call her my friend in her own right.

Most of the names – where known – of those at the
Twyford Allotments, Twyford Parish Council and any

other locations have remained unchanged. I would like to thank *everybody* I have come into contact with in the course of writing this book, eponymous, anonymous or pseudonymous, for their friendship, advice, generosity and sense of community.

My most heartfelt gratitude and love goes to my (for want of a better word) girlfriend, Jacqueline Watson. Her unflinching loyalty, remarkable patience, unfathomable tolerance, pragmatic counsel, unquestionable love and infectious enthusiasm have been, and continue to be, an extraordinary inspiration to me.

Finally, I would like to extend a special thank you to Andy Bostock at Gillon Aitken for initially digging the plot, as well as to my agent, Mary Pachnos and my editor, Ingrid Connell, who have both proved invaluable and incisive when it has come to weeding it. Were it not for these three people's foresight and belief in this book, it would be igniting the pea-sticks by now.

Robin Shelton
Twyford
August 2005

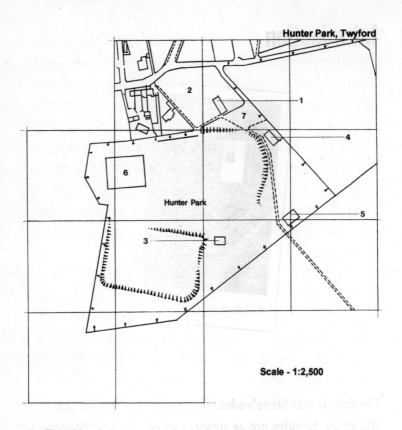

Hunter Park, Twyford

Hunter Park

Scale - 1:2,500

1. The plot
2. Parish allotments
3. The old pavillion
4. The new pavillion
5. Play area
   (including sandpit)
6. Tennis courts
7. Car park

Boundary - fence

Boundary - hedge

Footpath

Slopes

Introduction

Finding the Plot

I'm sure it was Steve's idea. When the rain is horizontal, the spade handles are as slippery as eels in a soapy bath and the mud is sticking to our boots like limpets hugging a wet rock he would, of course, hotly deny that he'd had anything to do with the inception of this patent madness. But the question of whose idea it was to take on a local disused vegetable plot is somewhat academic now, because take it on we did.

The allotments, which divide up just under an acre of

land, snooze quietly in a shallow hollow immediately to the north of Hunter Park, Twyford – a sleepy little place full of birdsong which is in turn approximately four miles south of Winchester, in Hampshire. The village hosts a friendly local pub run by a landlord who evidently knows his beer, and a cracking shop and coffee house which is run by people who obviously know their food. The combined capacity of these two establishments, along with the parquet-floored village hall, could probably, at a squeeze, accommodate all 1,400 of the village's inhabitants. To us, Twyford also serves as a starting point for a labyrinth of secret walks that we can cajole our dogs around when the world is too busy, noisy or both. Hunter Park itself, our local and absurdly idyllic recreation area, comprises a cricket square, two tennis courts and a football pitch arranged on a terrace cut into the incline of what used to be agricultural land until 1964 when Mr Hunter, a local farmer, donated it to the local council. From what I can ascertain, this was less to do with altruism than it was with the ground being next to impossible to cultivate by means of tractor and plough. Whichever, the backdrop to our story could only have been made more quintessentially 'English' had a couple of vicars eating crustless cucumber sandwiches and playing croquet been thrown in for good measure.

The real answer to the sometimes thorny question of exactly which of us it was that first suggested allotment husbandry probably suffered a fate similar to that of the beer cans whose contents had made both of us believe that it was a good idea in the first place, and our late-night discussions of our self-sufficient scheme have probably been recycled into an amiable, rambling chat about fly-fishing. It was early spring, and due to some relatively mild but nonetheless unpleasant depression, I had been off work (teaching in an art college) for a few months and Steve, my neighbour and a man I am lucky enough to call 'friend', had a job which was slowly driving him to a similar place. So, in a warm haze of cold beer, we decided that we would become gardeners. We both walked past the allotments fairly frequently, and both confessed to having, on occasion, found ourselves with half a mind to enquire about having a dig. Gluing these two halves together with sticky Belgian lager proved enough motivation for me, some time during May – possibly June – to call our local parish councillor and arrange to meet her with a view to reclaiming our very own Eden.

The task of finding out who to contact about the project was left to me largely by virtue of the fact that I had little else to do at the time except attempt to glue together those pieces of my life which had spent the previous year or so falling about my ears, but also because Steve is from Devon, and consequently often finds it difficult to make himself understood in this part of the country. Eventually, I tracked down a lady going by the very splendid name of Patricia Pottinger – had I tried to conjure up a more fitting name for a lady of whom one enquires about allotments in rural Hampshire, I don't feel I could have bettered this. We met at the allotments at the time arranged, although I cannot recall the date. However, I do remember the day being warm and quite green. As I lightly shook her bony and slender hand, I greeted her as 'Mrs Pottinger', innately sensing that 'Patricia' might be considered a little forward, and 'Pat' downright common. She was a charming lady with immaculate, sculpted silver-white hair, an elegant demeanour and a thin, blue, quilted body-warmer, quite possibly with a pair of secateurs snugly tucked inside the pocket. Steve had entrusted the choice of plots to me, as at the appointed time he was busy fulfilling his role as a care worker for the mentally disabled. Before I went, though, we agreed on one criterion: get the one that needs least doing to it.

When Mrs Pottinger showed me the two available, abandoned, plots, I surveyed them critically. The first was roughly 30 feet square with an oddly shaped and off-puttingly large bump in the middle of it, looking suspiciously as if somebody had buried a dead llama there. This plot was also covered in a carpet of surly and recalcitrant-looking weeds. The alternative, two plots to the east, was about 50 feet by 30 feet and festooned with grasses and other assorted vegetation so wild that Ray Mears may have found it intimidating. This one it was, then – I was sure that Steve would fully concur that we were far more capable of digging up a living jungle than we were of exhuming a rotting llama. Before making my final decision, I spent some time weighing up variables such as light, aspect, drainage, access, soil pH and size, before remembering that the only one of these I had any idea about whatsoever was the last one. So I went for the biggest which, by happy coincidence, also happened to be the one which was flat and therefore llama-free. This plot was also, I deduced, more fertile – why else would there be more stuff growing on it? The answer to this, of course, has a direct relationship to the amount of time since anyone put a fork in it. I was still a little concerned that Steve had not had the chance to see the plot before we committed ourselves, but Mrs Pottinger seemed keen to impress on me the fact that the chances of snapping up one of these allotments were, as she did not put it, as rare as rocking-horse crap.

Mrs Pottinger informed me in the gentlest way possible that the privilege of clearing this piece of wasteland only to realize that we hate gardening and never want to touch it again was going to cost us ten bloody pounds. Every bloody year. Steve and I had already agreed that we would split any and all costs and/or harvests right down the middle. Five bloody pounds, then. Each. Every bloody year. Steve took it remarkably well:

'Twenty bloody quid!'

There's one born every minute. Every fifty-nine seconds in Devon.

'I didn't think it was too b—'

'That's ten bloody quid each!'

'I know, but just thi—'

'Every bloody year!'

'Yeah, but when you work out how mu—'

'Nah, that's fine, mate, whatever.'

Later that day, we wandered up to survey our new territory, hands in pockets. I gave a proud sweep of my arms as soon as we were standing at the prow of the plot. I could sense that Steve's excitement at the prospect of conquering our own frontier mirrored my own.

'How the bloody hell are we gonna get all that crap out of there?'

I knew he would understand. Just to make sure, I pointed at the other plot.

'I know, but look, there's a dead lla—'

'Nah – that's fine, mate, honestly. Looks good. When shall we start?'

In terms of actually doing any physical work on the plot, the answer to this largely rhetorical question was to be 'mid-September-ish', but I do remember Steve and I spending most of the summer of that year discussing, at length and in great detail, topics such as exactly what needed to happen to the plot, how big it was, how fantastic it would be to have a shed and how much better it would be if we had a clue what we were doing. I also spent a good deal of time trying to involve my two children – Gabriel, then eight years old, and Dylan, five – in the project in an attempt to bore them as rigid as my late father did me a generation ago when he used to harp on about tools and mud and germination; but, after their mock-yawns and rolled eyeballs, I just had to hope that they would become enthused in a way similar to that in which I had – in their own time, on their own terms and with a couple of cans of lager inside them.

We decided that our first priority was, reasonably obviously, the removal of everything on the plot which we did not want or could not name (i.e. all of it), followed by weeding, digging over and/or squaring up some individual beds. We made an abortive attempt to hack at the largest bed with some hand-shears, two forks and a bucketful of bloody-mindedness. This area was top of the list primarily by virtue of the fact that it was the only bed we could find at the time, not to mention that we were more than a little scared by the potential diversity and/or ferocity of the fauna harboured by the remainder.

The possession of a large, noisy and potentially very dangerous machine changed all that, though. Just as soon as we had worked out where to find the 'on' switch of the petrol strimmer (which Steve had borrowed from a colleague at work) we cut through the scrub as easily, as a lecturer of mine once delightfully put it, as pissing into snow. Doing this revealed a number of things. First, that the plot indeed comprised a recognizable, if random and irregular sprawl of separate beds. It also laid bare an assortment of rubble, rusting metal and unidentifiable rotting wood. There was a very forlorn-looking and entirely unserviceable compost bin which had evidently been fabricated by hand (just the one by the look of it) from sheets of corrugated steel and wooden posts. Presumably, when it had been made, it had been rectangular, the steel had not been rusty and the wood not rotten. It now looked as if it had been hastily constructed by a Salvador Dali obsessed by compost bins, not clocks. We had also inherited our very own wasp-magnet in the shape of a large blackcurrant bush, which we were not sure was a curse or a blessing. We decided that we would either remove it or not after extensive periods of weighing up the pros and cons of both. In other words, we would dig it up if we felt like it, if we could and if we got that far. But deemed as serviceable – if only temporarily – were a large green plastic compost bin, an orange bucket and three pieces of wood nailed together and sunk into the ground in parody of a bench.

Our resources in terms of tools were equally, er, challenging. As well as the previously mentioned shears and two forks (one of which was bought, along with a spade, for ten pounds, the other a piece of flotsam from the sunken ship of my marriage), we had, erm . . . we also had a, er, a, had, erm, a thing. No, wait – actually, I think I lent that to someone a few years ago. So that was about it. Oh, we did have two sticks with some string wrapped around them to mark out a straight line and a large stainless steel flask which I had salvaged from the local tip. We reckoned this would be enough to get us started, though – we could mark out a bed, cut around it and dig it over. We could even stop for tea when it all got to be too much for us. And we both agreed that there was little point in spending money which neither of us had on new equipment which we probably didn't know how to use, until we were sure that we were going to see the project through. At the time, we simply wanted to be seduced and guided by a set of arcane and as yet unknown principles and processes. Not only did we not know 'who' got us into this or precisely 'when', but, at the outset, we were also at a bit of a loss as to 'why'.

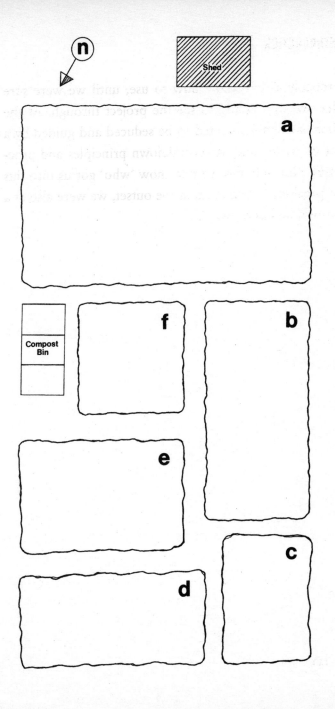

Our Allotment

Gabriel Shelton, aged nine

Vegetables, fruit, soil and shed,
Water, compost and Charlie's bed,
Spades, shovels, buckets and forks,
Magazines, footballs and a few cranky dorks.
Dad, Steve, Dylan and me,
Eddie, Charlie and a bucket for pee.
Sweetcorn, peas, beans and spuds,
Marigolds, carrots and a few little buds.
Now it is time for my poem to end –
Let's hope good weather is what summer will send.

1 Preparing the Ground

Pointy and Painful

21 September

'If laang, straight, reliable carrots is what you's aafter,' the rubber bung at the end of Ken's stick circled authoritatively a few inches in front of my face, 'then it's gorra be Autumn King!' The stick stopped circling and instead prodded the air in time with the last two words, as if to underline and punctuate them.

Neither Steve nor I had the heart or inclination to

tell Ken – a taut, gaunt and elderly man with a demeanour not so much stooped as conquered – that we had, in fact, planned on stumpy, twisted carrots which we couldn't trust as far as we could grow.

'Nice one, Ken – we'll remember tha—'

'You growin' 'tatoes?' I had never seen a walking stick squint inquisitively before. Steve and I exchanged shrugs and glances. How should we know? We'd only just realized that potatoes didn't grow on trees. We both nodded anyway.

'Yeah.'

'Desiree.' The stick was defiant.

'Sorry?'

'Only thing worth growin', Desiree,' confirmed Ken.

'Don't you even know that?' waggled the rubber bung.

With that, Ken and his stick mumbled and trundled their way over to their own plot which, even to our novice eyes, looked unlikely to support anything as regal as Autumn Kings, or as alluring as Desirees. Old codger. What the bloody hell did he know?

We had planted ourselves on the bank at the top of our allotment for a well earned tea break, as we had been digging solidly for a good five minutes, and had both started to simper at roughly the same time. Today was our first day's work on our new venture; our first skirmish in the war against bland, chemical-laden super-market produce. Our first pace on a journey which would hopefully take us to previously unobtainable levels of natural harmony. It was also our first day of probably many more of arriving at the plot and scratching our heads in puzzlement as to exactly how we were ever going to grow anything on it and why we were even bothering to do so. One reason, for me at least, is to give me something to doodle about in my journal – one of today's entries reads:

At the allotment. An allotment diary perhaps? A year working the soil. 'Allotted Time.' Pulling accordion earthworms from their loamy slumber. Desiree potatoes and Autumn King carrots, apparently.

The intended outcome of today's venture up to the plot was less agricultural than symbolic. It was in very much an animal sense that we wanted to go up there and mark out our territory – so we delineated our first rectangle of ground by urinating on to the grass before starting to square it up.

As it happened, though, we actually managed to get a reasonable amount done today. To ease the pain of our toil, Steve had made a flask of coffee and had brought along his wind-up radio, so we enjoyed a thoroughly civilized afternoon of making a fair attempt to weed and dig the top bed of the plot, which is about 30 feet by 15 feet and, we have concluded, destined to be potatoes. We started with this bed as the rest of the plot is thick with grasses, fruit shrubs and metal-rusting experiments, and there really is only so far you can go with two bent forks, five pounds' worth of spade, two sticks with some string wrapped round them and a pair of hand-shears about as sharp and effective as a peeled banana.

It may also be relevant to clarify here that Steve and I currently have absolutely no idea about gardening whatsoever, except for knowing which end of the fork is which. And we only found this out through the pointy and painful trial and error method. Steve's career path has led him from clotted-cream fudge taster to carer and social worker via a well-intentioned but ill-advised stint in the army, and I have similarly managed to avoid anything remotely horticultural by teaching surfing for a few years, then getting a degree in Jewellery Design before spending the following six years staring at both it and the rest of my life and not knowing exactly what to do with either of them. Steve and I met, about eight months ago, as a result of a domestic crisis on my part. My ex-girlfriend had recently moved out, and taken her vacuum cleaner with her. There are some very politically incorrect jokes regarding what happens when your wife or girlfriend leaves you, but I shall rise above them. The house-work did mount up, though, most noticeably with an increase in the amount of dust and hair lying around. I was pathetically poor, so even buying a dustpan and brush would have been a major consideration – I had to borrow a vacuum cleaner from somebody. The only problem I had was that, apart from my children, for whom I am responsible for roughly half the year, and ex-wife, who lives in Winchester and tends to them for the other half, I didn't actually know anybody. What remained of my 'social' life had just vacated the prem-ises and I had spent the previous six months being at times genuinely afraid of leaving the flat.

However, this was a good day, so I turned left out of the drive and ambled up the road, listening for the whooshing whine of domestic labour like a lonely drunkard shuffling along a road listening for the cheer and coloured lights of a party. Strangely, no one seemed to be doing the hoovering at the precise moment I was looking for that very apparatus – luckily, though, some-one only two doors up had very thoughtfully parked a large and solid-looking motorbike in their drive. I like bikes. Therefore, by and large, I tend to get on with those who ride them. The front door was open, so I tapped and shouted, 'Hello!'

A gently handsome chap came lolloping down the

stairs in his slippers, with his mousy ponytail bobbing behind him. He smiled warmly.

'Hello, mate. What can I do for you?'

Another question to which I still do not know the answer. So far it's been a privilege to try to find out, though.

We may not know an awful lot about gardening, but we have formulated two basic principles: number one states that whatever we need to know and cannot find in the bookshelves of the local charity shops can be gleaned from my mother, who has been gardening for centuries. Principle number two is based on the belief that, well, stuff just grows, doesn't it? In fact, we are armed with more than that; we are both emboldened by our conviction that, somehow, the saviour of our sanity lies dormant under those grasses. Or perhaps that was what that big lump was on the other available plot and I've chosen the wrong one after all. I suppose we both feel an abstract desire to become more involved in and connected with the cyclic processes of nature, and in some senses 'play God' of our own vegetable world, perhaps because we both feel a similar lack of control over which direction our respective real ones are going. And, although what I know about gardening can be written on a plant label large enough to fit the words 'bugger' and 'all' onto, I can at least remember a peculiar feeling of satisfaction from childhood, when I would help my father to plant potatoes. He would let me plunge into the soil with the dobber, or dibber, or nobber, or whatever it was called – his was a truncated, tapered and sparrow-breast-brown spade handle, cleft and bent and worm-ridden. He would give me a stick to mark off the spaces between the holes, and I would dob, dib or nob at these measured intervals. His gawky frame – only as old as mine is now, but bent and twisted by the cruel contortions of premature rheumatoid arthritis – followed me with precarious egg boxes laden with tentacled tubers, and he would drop one into each hole, interring it with an incongruously deft shuffle of his aching feet. Meanwhile his thick, rough sponge of a beard would talk to me about potatoes, gardening, life cycles and all manner of other things which meant nothing whatsoever to me then. All I cared about was the grubby 2p piece I got for every hole I dobbed, dibbed or nobbed.

I also grew some potatoes as a grown-up once, all by myself. Well, nearly all by myself. During the spring of 1996, under instruction from my mother, I buried a dozen or so spuds which had gone past their best, in a disused patch of soil. A couple of months or so later, proving beyond reasonable doubt principle number one, I uprooted, if not a bounty, then at least more than I had put in. This happened during a relatively dry spell, throughout which the only time they got watered was when I remembered, elucidating, and possibly even begetting, principle number two.

5 November

I have become aware, over the last month or so, that this level of knowledge ('Mum knows, stuff grows') may not be quite enough to get us through, so I have drawn up a template – what I have dubbed a 'veg fact sheet' – on which I can condense some of the information culled from my growing range of charity-shop bargain books, as an aide-memoire. Realistically, these documents are going to be the only way two sieve-brains like us have a snowball in hell's chance of growing anything edible.

So, keen, experienced and knowledgeable gardeners we may not be. Luckily on that first day, though, we met a man who says he is. Ken, it transpires, knows all it is feasible to know about allotment husbandry. In fact Ken, extraordinarily enough, apparently knows pretty much everything about everything. The few things that Ken does not know could be written on a plant label just large enough for the words '*sod*' and '*all*' to be squeezed onto. Ken's alarmingly expressive walking stick seems to be part perambulatory aid, part gesturing device, part weapon and part bullshit diviner. The disturbing thing about him is not so much the way he waggles this stick (more of a branch, really) towards you at roughly solar plexus height in a gesture similar to the manner in which some wave an admonishing finger. No, it is more the fact that, until he starts to brandish it, it looks for all the world as if he is thoroughly incapable of standing without it. From then on, it is impossible to talk to Ken without internally conjecturing on which way he is going to topple, whether he will he miss you on his way down and, most importantly, whether you will be able to suppress the laughter already welling inside you at the thought of it. Steve and I have deduced that this stick, although not strictly necessary for walking, is ultimately some kind of spade-placebo – Ken spent so many of his formative years digging, raking, hoeing, etc., that he simply feels unbalanced without something to connect his hands to the ground.

While we have sat at the top of the plot, sharing a mug of tea, Ken has very often regaled us with pearls of wisdom regarding carrots, potatoes and weed-wrestling techniques. He has also recounted numerous and often seemingly endless tales of wartime allotment gardening too involved and/or incomprehensible to repeat here, but suffice to say that Ken is one of a diminishing band of people who feel not one ounce of self-consciousness when commencing a sentence with the words 'during the war'.

Violence and confrontation do have their place, though – and it is in achieving horticultural harmony. In our case, this meant waging outright war on the battalions of weeds and grasses encamped on our land. We have tried hacking our way through these, mainly on the bottom two-thirds of the plot, with our 'compact' range of hand tools, but have been held back by a barrage of greenery effectively sticking their thumbs in their ears and waggling their fingers while blowing raspberries and sing-songing 'nya na na-na na' at us. So, on a visit to the allotment a couple of weeks ago, we took with us a large and robust petrol-driven strimmer which Steve had managed to cadge from a work colleague. We had considered firing up my flame-thrower, but decided otherwise because the only service it has seen since I bought it from Helston tip for a fiver two years ago is in the capacity of fuel can for lighting large and primitive fires in my incinerator. In comparison, the strimmer was an elegant, accurate and refined tool. More importantly, it was a little less likely to kill us. Only a little, however, so we took all relevant safety precautions. Namely, we wore long trousers, squinted a little to stop chunks of grass, soil and other eye-seeking missiles from gouging our sight from us, and Steve made sure that his roll-ups had very nearly gone out before refuelling.

Two tanks of a 25:1 petrol/oil mix and a lot of noise, fumes and maniacal laughter later, Steve and I surveyed our newly shaved rectangle. It actually looked as if we had done much more than we had – an effect to effort ratio of at least 25:1 – in much the same way that it looks like more work to give a crew-cut to a hippy than to a squaddie. What mattered was that we had a roughly rectangular area in which we could discern an irregular pattern of beds, cut by the previous incumbent. We put what had formerly been the swaying, vertical stems of unnamed grasses in a distinctly horizontal and unceremonious pile, along with various other organic bits and pieces, in the inherited tangle of bent steel and rotting wood that we have temporarily and somewhat grandiosely named the 'compost bin'.

Now that we had a clear and more manageable plot and had paced it at roughly 50 feet by 30 feet, we could start to plan where we were going to arrange beds, paths and seating as well as our real reason for having an allotment in the first place: the currently hypothetical shed. The large bed to the south of the plot – which, being the first one in which we put our forks, we have imaginatively labelled bed 'a' – actually consists of one large and one small area, the latter being only about 2 feet wide, running roughly north to south. We have decided to keep this small bed for garlic or perhaps some herbs, because digging up the grass path between the two strikes us as a pain in the arse too far when there are more pressing things to be dealt with.

Because the newly discovered arrangement of beds is discernible (even if only by virtue of the weeds growing in them being slightly more sparse than those growing on the paths), and because rearranging them seems like a pointless waste of time, we have decided to stick with what we have been given. While we were committing green genocide with the strimmer, we also 'cut back' the currant bush which resides halfway down the east side, but have decided to keep it on the grounds of continuity and further laziness. The remainder of the plot consists of five further beds of varying sizes, plus space for the shed and possibly a seating area for summer barbecues and winter sulking.

Four days ago, for the first time in a while, we went to the plot with the intention of squaring and tidying up a bed or two. We were armed with the essential kit – big flask of tea (from the local tip, stainless steel, 1.5 litre capacity, no handle, £2), forks, graph-paper plot plan and, of course, our two sticks wrapped with string, which will prove useful for all sorts of jobs such as marking out beds, and delineating rows down which we will drag our hoe (when we have one). But they served very well then in assisting us in marking out two sides of our rectangle at a time (with the cunning assistance of a further, found, stick acting as a corner marker) along which we split the turf with the spade. Neither Steve nor I is in any way an accomplished digger, and it was not long before one of us (almost certainly him, great wimp) suggested we break for tea. My back was groaning to such an extent that I found it virtually impossible, once we had sat on our 'bench' for ten minutes or so, to stand up again. I motioned to him that I'd be with him just as soon as I had spent a while scribbling in my journal. It says:

1 November

A day at the allotment with Steve. At about this time last week we planned to do some digging today, and I have found myself curiously looking forward to it since then. Today we have set ourselves the target of finishing off bed 'a' and starting on bed 'b'. Along with the rest of the plot, this latter has become overgrown with a combination of wild grasses and weeds, underpinned by scores of unidentified flower bulbs huddled together like small netted onions.

ALLOTTED TIME

A hard afternoon's digging (is there another sort?), punctuated by hefty swigs of tannin-laden tea from my perpetually musty flask.

   Initially we had the allotments to ourselves. The air hung thick, damp and still. Greying. The kind of day which doesn't rain, but still moistens. The resonant drone of the propeller-driven planes which lumbered low overhead, Southampton-bound from the north – Manchester, perhaps, or Glasgow – sounded as if they were dubbed behind the studio fog of some generic 1950s' Hollywood B-movie full of impossible love and improbable endings. As we turned our clods of damp, sticky and rocky soil, revealing the startling white-yellow stems of buried bulbs, and startled juicy purple earthworms – our own soil conditioners – I couldn't help smiling at the surprising and new-found pleasure that a combination of physical toil, almost literal connectedness with the earth and easy, trusted companionship brings. Life is good sometimes, even in autumn – a season I have come to deeply mistrust as the harbinger of winter doom. During a break, earned by reaching the end of bed 'a', I indulged in a wander about. I noticed more photographs I'd like to take – the thin, bowed red strips of fallen sycamore leaf stems, complementary to but shocking against the stubborn green of lopped fir branches, and the gloriously opaque statement of delicate net curtains drawn across the window of the shed – all square and burnt sienna – which Ted, keeper of the allotment next to ours and true font of all gardening knowledge, has recently moved from his plot to the bank just above it.

   The digging has been heavy going, which is a little like saying that the earth was brown. Unravelling the string, and releasing the two wooden pegs it is attached to at either end, we marked out in stages the rectangle of what is to be bed 'b', which we guessed, after much sucking of teeth, kicking of rocks and forgetting of tape measures, to be about 10 feet by 20 feet. We dug around this edge, then worked inwards. The moss and assorted weeds have formed a thick, tangled green carpet reluctant to release its grip on the sticky soil, much of which we did not bother to separate, and instead chucked it on the compost heap as it was. We weren't sure whether this was the right thing to do or not, but it seemed reasonable by virtue of it being the right colour. Must remember to check this later with Mum, who has an uncanny knack of always being right when I want her to be. After we had dug about two-thirds of the bed, we stopped for a tea break, and as we sat, the number of souls on the allotments was doubled by the arrival of Ted and his grandson, whom he had brought along in order to demonstrate to him the finer arts of pyrotechnics.

Ted is, at a guess, between sixty-five and seventy years old. Unlike Ken, he needs no means of artificial support for either walking or conversation, as both seem to come very naturally. His leathery (even in this gloom of oncoming winter) arms have been cured and tanned by a lifetime of sunshine and soil. He also appears to be some kind of composite 'ideal grandfather' – the sort that brings his ten-year-old grandson to the plot in order to teach him how to light a good fire and has a tank-top stitched to every shirt, each with its sleeves rolled squarely and permanently to just past the elbow. No doubt he has a dustless shelf of model vintage cars at home and a selection of chocolates and toffees in his pocket. On top of this, according to what seemed to be a reliable source, he is 'the best gardener in Twyford'. And us two numpties have got the plot next to his. Fan-bloody-tastic – someone who can really show us up. Smashing bloke, though. We had met during a previous foray to the plot, during which we had really warmed to him – there are some people you instinctively know you will get along with. They are the ones who say things such as, 'It's grand to see some youngsters on the plots.' I haven't been called a 'youngster' since I didn't want to be one.

While we were chatting the other day, Ted eyed our tarpaulin which we had laden with clumpy sods of soil and tangled weeds, having already filled the compost bin to overflowing. His Hampshire drawl is less pro-nounced than Ken's and, also unlike Ken, Ted does not deem it necessary to shout from two paces.

'What you doin' wi' that lot?'

We hadn't thought that far. All we'd concerned our-selves with was making a big brown rectangle on our plot. As for what was going to happen to the stuff we were clearing from it, well, this constituted forward planning. Not something entirely familiar to either of us. We told him that we had no idea, and did he have any suggestions? After adjusting his tweed flat-cap left to right then front to back, he gestured towards a triangle of scrub to the south-east corner of his plot.

'That bit o' land there ain't bein' used – you can chuck 'im on there. Oh, by the way, 'ave you met Ken yet?'

This last was accompanied by what I am convinced was a smile, along with a brighter than usual twinkle in the eye.

'Briefly, yeah.' Steve and I exchanged one-eyed looks and half-mouthed smiles.

'Jus' wondrin'.'

Ted turned towards his net-curtained shed, presumably to fettle with tools or perform a rain incantation. Sometimes 'jus' wondrin'' is all that is required.

We grunted our gratitude for Ted's offer of allowing us to dump our crap on his land and strode as purposefully as possible towards our tarpaulin. We then proceeded to threaten bed-blocking of the local hospital's traction unit by attempting to drag approximately 130 square feet's worth of weeds, stones and topsoil to the designated area. Eventually, we admitted defeat – or at least compromise – and decided to accomplish this in somewhere between 2 and 15 loads.

Once we had been galvanized by a) emptying the tarpaulin, b) seeing the result of our efforts and c) the presence of a man who is possibly older – and who certainly looks healthier – than both of us put together, working the adjacent plot, we got stuck into the remainder of the bed with a good deal of enthusiasm. Because of this new-found zeal, and because we were mindful not to put too much stuff on the tarpaulin before heaving it over to the top of Ted's plot, it wasn't too long before we were again clasping two corners each and dragging it, like a lead balloon, then depositing its contents by rolling and tumbling it over, kicking it and shouting at it.

Eventually, we were faced with the previously unlikely prospect of being finished. As we were throwing the last of the weeds onto the sheet, we spotted Ken thundering down the path – recognizable immediately by his three-legged gait and his unique sense of purpose for no apparent reason. Steve and I have suggested, between ourselves, that Ken is approaching 900 years old and no longer gardens using rusting tools and grubby fingers, but by utilizing mind-control techniques. This is the only logical conclusion in view of the fact that no one has ever seen him lift a finger up here in the last three months. Plenty of sticks, but no fingers.

As we dragged the tarp past the top of Ted's plot, we

alerted him to the presence of the mystic one. Ted scuttled behind his shed to rearrange his beanpoles as Steve and I threw the dregs of what we had spent the last three hours uprooting on top of everything else there (more weeds, two old pizza boxes and a sock). By this point, Ken was within shouting distance, his stick evidently now redundant for walking purposes and being used more in the capacity of jousting lance. Ken is like a tractor – surprisingly fast when you are standing still and he is coming towards you.

'What you doin' on my land?'

Steve and I were holding two corners of empty tarpaulin each, looking down at our shuffling shoes like two schoolboys caught playing conkers in class.

'Er, sorry, Ken, we . . . erm, well, we . . . er . . . we . . . just thought it was common ground.'

Neither of us had either the guts or the indecency to incriminate Ted, so Ken continued to huff and puff and point his stick at the underused and overgrown patch of earth which, as a matter of record, is actually nowhere near his plot. After a few moments of this, Ted reappeared from his pole-jiggling and said, somewhat sheepishly, that it had been his suggestion that we dump our clods there, as he was under the reasonable impression that the piece of land was his, seeing as it happened to be adjacent to his plot. He had made this assumption when he took over his plot only a couple of months before we started on ours. The bung at the end of Ken's stick, which probably first saw active service at some time during the reign of Henry the First, once more made reluctant contact with the soil as its owner reminded Ted of the Scalene Triangles of Wasteland Act of 1723, which he, Ken, had not only read and understood, but also written at the age of 597.

Steve and I were, for a while, a little concerned that we would be forced to spend a further half-day carting our unwanted greenery over to someone else's unused and useless piece of land, but Ken and Ted managed to resolve things in the way that elderly men sometimes do – by gently bickering about something else until the matter in hand is forgotten. That's what I assume happened, anyway – Steve and I sloped off to whinge over a pint in the Phoenix before we were asked to do anything else.

14 November

Up at the plot, dodging the rain. Or, in fact, not dodging it but getting well and truly pissed on by it. Still, better than getting pissed off, which I am not. Not sure where Steve's got to – I saw his bike at the front of his place this morning as I was taking the boys to school, but by the time I had got back it was gone. Didn't think he was working today. Whatever, he's not digging, for which there is no excuse. I shall hit him squarely with my spade the moment I next see him. I wanted to get up here today no matter what as I felt a sense of urgency to sort out the compost situation. We inherited half a bin-load of decent rotted grass (but not much else of any use) from the previous incumbent, on top of which we have piled some of the turfs resulting from our previous attempts at finding some soil on beds 'a' and 'b'. Steve and I have also been saving all our kitchen scraps to supplement this measly offering. However, we have decided, for reasons which escape me right now, that it would be an excellent idea to move the compost somewhere else. To do this, we needed first to eject all the contents of the old bin, which I have just done, and put all the compostable stuff in the other, green plastic bin. On top of this, I have also dumped a bin bag full of wet and rotting leaves gathered from the other side of the park. Leaf mould, as Steve learned recently, is very good for the condition of the soil and although these aren't mouldy yet, they soon will be when the orange peel and bits of onion skin have their grubby bacterial way with them. I also found out recently, to my under-standable delight, that urine can be used both as an effective compost activator (neat) and as an excellent general fertilizer (diluted 1:10 with water). So Steve and I can now, quite literally and with full justification, come up here and piss on our territory. Wonderful.

18 November

At the plot. A morning as crisp and translucent as a crease in a sheet of tracing paper. The sun, like a smudge of pale yellow paint behind it, was approaching its measly zenith.

Ted arrived as I was coaxing Charlie, my short-haired, wall-eyed and brick-brained lurcher – sleek with sweat and lolling tongued – back into the car. I figured that he'd be glad of the rest – there are only so many sticks one dog can chase, after all. Ted was not staying for long, he said, but just stopping off on his way through to the tip, the destination for some weeds and rubble he dug up yesterday. As he was loading up, he gestured towards the lopped branches of the currant bushes, the stumps of which I vowed I would dig up today after organizing the compost.

'You can put those on that pile, if you like.' He nodded towards a jumble of combustibles to the far side of his shed which we have begun to eye from our wet, exposed bench with a level of jealousy bordering on the criminal. I offered to bring up my incinerator, quite possibly in an attempt to curry favour in the shelter department, but again there was a twinkle in one of his blue eyes, and an upturned corner of his mouth as he assured me that this will not be necessary, as he plans to burn it as it lies. Maybe it is Ted who is the pyromaniac after all, and his grandson, 'for whom' he has lit more than one fire since the beginning of the month, is merely a foil for these tendencies. Maybe he doesn't even like gardening much, but an allotment gives him plenty of excuses for setting light to stuff.

After Ted had gone, I started to dig up the shrubs currently (no pun intended) standing between us and some neat rows of onions. If I said that it was hard going, I fear I may once again be stating the bleeding obvious, but somehow sharing the pain makes it easier. However, as anyone who has ever spent any time hacking a stout and perfectly good plant to bits using only brute force, ignorance and a spade will tell you, it is extremely satisfying when the last rope of the root system gives way. I stumbled backwards with the cartwheeling arms and overbalancing surprise of sudden compliance after stubborn resistance and, not for the first time, found myself wondering whether it is possible to work out the calorific input/output equation of a given vegetable patch and whether the amount of energy supplied ever even comes close to that which is put in. How many carrots would I need to eat to replace the energy expended in cultivating the ground in which I grew them? Probably enough to allow me to garden in the dark. As I lifted the roots, I shook as much of the clinging soil from them as I deemed necessary, or as much as I could be bothered, then hump-thudded them onto the tarpaulin, where small lumps of earth and rock sprayed and scattered themselves over the blue rectangle.

Just after I had butchered the largest of the stumps, Three-Legged Ken arrived and regaled me with some random stories. First, he informed me of the intricacies of his daughter's lawn-mower's safety switch, which led him, tenuously but somehow seamlessly, to an anecdote concerning his gas boiler, and consequently to the relative merits or otherwise of the central-heating systems of most of the village. As I listened, it dawned on me that Ken does not require or recognize the same sentence structure as us mere mortals; he mixes up his own cacophony of verbs, adjectives, nouns, pronouns and adverbs with a unique blend of grunts, clicks and whirrs, into a kind of linguistic jazz. The strange thing is that I can still understand if not every word he is saying, then at least the general thrust of every point he is making.

I can still hear the music, even if I don't know the score. It also struck me that, as far as conversation with Ken is concerned, there are three governing principles:

1 Do not attempt to say anything. There is no point, as Ken has telepathic capabilities. It's either that, or he is as deaf as a post. A further possibility – that he really doesn't give a toss about what you have to say – has been mooted, but I find this hard to believe.

2 There is no need to concentrate on what Ken is saying. Listen in the same manner as he speaks, i.e. entirely on your own terms. Trying to follow a conversation with Ken is, anyway, a frustrating affair, because as soon as you have boarded his train of thought, he will have alighted and be heading for an entirely different platform, possibly even station. All that is required is to nod and make the correct facial expressions at roughly the right time.

3 Finally, largely due to maxims 1 and 2, a conversation with Ken is not a conversation at all. It is, in fact, an good excuse to stop digging for a while.

2 The Shed

Places to Potter

24 November

We have started making our shed. There had been talk
of whether doing so would prove somewhat futile once
we had decided that gardening was a stupid waste of
time, suitable only for those with mental health issues
or learning disabilities. However, a slippery and precarious arrangement of random planks masquerading
under the name of 'bench' is no place for frontiersmen

such as Steve and me to drink tea and discuss beans. We need a slippery and precarious arrangement of random planks masquerading under the name of 'shed' for that.

But it is more than that – a shed is also somewhere to sit, out of the rain, with a cup of steaming leathery tea and a true friend. It is somewhere to hear, amongst the cake jokes and pigeon updates, news of the latest England batting demise on *Test Match Special*. It is somewhere to dither, potter, fettle and fiddle, whilst getting your hands suitably grubby. It is a refuge for those frequent occasions when the world has too many people in it, and when other buildings or spaces seem too cold and expansive – inside a shed all dimensions can be touched without moving; it is more human in scale, and consequently more womb-like. It is an environment which is entirely under your own terms and control – no planning consent is required for a shed (no doubt Ken will tell us otherwise). More important, it is shelter; and the best shelter, as anyone who has put up a tent and climbed into it will testify, is that which you have fashioned yourself.

We have scoured the local papers and made a few phone calls but cannot seem to find anyone who is willing to sell us a shed for less than either of us would currently be willing or able to spend on a car – therefore we must make our own, using whatever materials we have lying around, or those which can be sourced either for nothing, or next to nothing, from the tip. To make life really interesting, we have decided that our budget for the project is to be ten pounds. Between us. I told Steve it would be twenty. Luckily, I have a garage full of odd lengths of timber and boxes of screws of various sizes, and Steven has one containing, amongst many other things he can neither name nor use, two old wooden garage doors and the timber from two disused pine bunk beds. These we 'disassembled' recently using a crowbar, a lump hammer and four steel toecaps, and I don't think that it will ever cease to amaze and enthral me how the prospect of violence towards an inanimate object can turn two relatively intelligent and sensitive men into drooling and brutal thugs.

So 21 November saw us stamping on my garage floor and blowing into our cupped hands to stave off the cold. Our aim for the day was to construct the base, utilizing some stout rectangular section pine I had lying around and some of the slats from the bunk beds. Also in our arsenal were an array of screws, some basic tools and a sketch of a shed drawn on graph paper in order to engender the false belief that we had any idea of what we were doing. Our specification for the shed was as follows: It must:

1 cost less than ten pounds,
2 be up before Christmas,
3 be big enough for us both to sit in at the same time in order to drink tea and talk bollocks,
4 look like a big box with a slopey top,
5 have a door,
6 and maybe a window.

Starting with the bottom seemed to make sense, so we laid out five lengths of 4 inch by 2 inch pine in the correct proportions for our base (6 feet by 4 feet). On top of these, and at right angles to them, we laid out the timber from the beds, screwing each piece into place as we did so. After a couple of hours or so of nudging, banging, screwing and grunting (now, now), we had in front of us a good approximation of what might pass as a shed floor. We kicked it and we jumped on it as we made primitive male-bonding noises involving the use of words such as 'solid', 'spot on' and 'lovely job' spoken in low, gruff Estuary English. We had begun.

When Lizzie, Steve's 'diamond geezer' of a wife craned her head around the door to tell us that soup and home-baked bread were both warm and on the table, we felt like brethren to the Amish barn-raisers. Which is remarkable, considering the truth of the matter was that we were what we usually are – a brace of clueless and atheistic halfwits who had just knocked together something which looked for all the world like a fairly substantial pallet, but with smaller gaps between the slats. Steve spoke first; 'Looks like a big pallet, doesn't it?'

He had a point. And we *had* spent an awfully long time producing something which we could have procured from any night-time lorry park. I tried to come up with something in reply which might distinguish our efforts.

'Yeah. But the gaps are smaller, look.'

'Good point, mate. Let's eat.'

One of the myriad reasons why it is impossible for me to even begin to dislike Steve is his capacity to make me feel as if I have some idea of what I am talking about when I know full well that I am blowing it out of my backside. When, as so often, it feels as if the world is full of people who are only too keen to tell you what you are doing wrong and when you are doing it, it is certainly edifying to share a part of my life with someone who seems completely oblivious to my incompetence. It's even better when they are about to give you lunch.

After we had slurped soup and drank tea, we decided that making the framework would be far too complicated, and instead opted to celebrate the completion of the base by getting sponge-wet dragging our two frankly

ambivalent dogs (Charlie – lurcher, brainless, and Eddie
– Jack Russell terrier, psychotic) around five miles of
soggy, but nonetheless spectacular, Hampshire.

Today, however, I carried on with the construction.
Another characteristic which endears Steve to me the
most is his often brutal, but somehow never insensitive,
honesty. I suppose it is an indication of the strength of
our friendship that, when I suggested we go vertical
in our shed-making, he told me that he truly couldn't
be bothered and fancied watching a video instead. He
added, somewhat unnecessarily, that if I wanted to carry
on without him then that was fine by him. I armed
myself with tools similar to those which helped fashion
the base, but with a much more purposeful-looking
drawing which I knocked up last night. This one was on
A2 paper and detailed, on a scale of 1:10, the lengths,
sections and angles required (as laid down by numbers
3 and 4 in our list of specifications). I had decided that
the shed should have a pent roof – one which sloped
from front to back – as opposed to an apex roof, whose
high point is in the middle, running from side to side.
This was because of the perceived, and therefore quite
possibly erroneous, gain in structural strength and rigid-
ity of the former, taking into account factors such as

prevailing wind, vector dynamics and torsional stresses. It was also because it struck me as being an awful lot easier to make.

The idea was to make two skeleton sides and a cross brace to connect them just under the roof, and the material of choice was a selection of lengths of 2 inch by 2 inch planed pine, or 'PAR' as those in the know and the low-cut trousers call it. This stuff is a legacy from an ill-advised and abortive attempt to make some kitchen cupboards for someone earlier in the year. A project which, with hindsight, I should never have taken on at all, but it takes more than a job which has never before been attempted to dissuade a penniless manic-depressive, in springtime, from saying 'yes' to pretty much anything. Still, caveat emptor and all that.

A surprisingly short time later I found myself in the ludicrous position of trying to hold two shed-frame sides and support one cross brace in place atop and between these, at the same time as looking at the whole in an attempt to get an idea of what the finished thing will look like. It was no use. I'll have to find a slot in my hectic schedule over the next few days to enlist Steve.

A successful day, then: the shed is now three-dimensionalized, the dog is exercised and the compost bin has been fertilized with the bottle of urine which I have been filling in the garage when I am too dirty or lazy or both to go up to the flat. Tomorrow, I think, we plan to dig again. I can't remember whether we agreed on tomorrow or the next day, and it's too late to call Stevie now to check. What I do know is that it is 1.15 a.m. and I am tired.

3 In Readiness for Sowing

stuff Grows, huh?

1 December

A new month, heralding what is usually, for me, the darkest of seasons in more ways than one. Yet still my mood seems buoyed by what I can only assume is the therapeutic nature of gardening – although I hesitate to use that word, as I can only really claim to have performed a tiny minority of the tasks required. Still, even these activities have given an entirely new sense of purpose to winter, and have made me realize, somewhat grudgingly, that this season is something of a necessary evil and that without it there would be no spring. During some of my more pronounced winter lows of previous years I have toyed with the idea of throwing it all in and moving somewhere near the equator – all that year-round light and heat and evenness – but now I suspect that I would simply find it dull. The smooth succession and balanced opposition of our seasons mirrors so much else about the human condition and our environment – the waxing and waning of the moon and its associated tidal rise and fall, the ebb and flow of our moods – even our own cyclic existence of coming from, and returning to, nothing. This is simply the natural state of things.

Besides, we have a celebration coming up in a few weeks – not the conspicuously materialistic treadmill that Christmas has become, but the real reason why Christianity hijacked this particular date from the pagans. It is the time of year when we are given back just a little bit of precious light each day. In twenty-one days, the shortest and darkest day of the year will be gone. Now that *is* an excuse for a turkey and a piss-up.

Right, I'm off to see Sue Harris, our hawk-like allotment society secretary, to pick up our seeds. 'Allotment society' is perhaps something of a misnomer – as far as

I'm aware there are no meetings (it's either that or we haven't been invited to any for some unfathomable reason), and 'joining' the 'society' seems to involve no more action on anyone's part than sticking an inquisitive fork into the soil of one of the plots. From what I can gather, the sole benefit of 'membership' is that we get our seeds at half retail price. I can't wait to get them growing, but from what I can gather it's a bit cold yet. I feel like an impetuous child waiting to open a half-known present. I wonder whether, as well as hinting that winter can be survived without entertaining thoughts of *permanent* darkness, gardening may also teach me a little patience.

I've just walked back home from Sue's house, expectantly clutching a satisfyingly thick and rattly wedge of seed packets wrapped in a brown paper bag and cinched with an elastic band the like of which I last saw being produced from an ACME box by Wile E. Coyote. A rundown of what we've got: carrots – Autumn King because we are scared of Ken's stick, and St Valery because in the catalogue they looked like the ones that Bugs Bunny eats (vivid orange and evenly tapered). Leeks – Firena and the oddly named Autumn Giant 3 – Rami. Onions – Bedfordshire Champion because it is 'a reliable cropper' and 'good for storing', and 'Brunswick' because they are red. We have swedes – Brora and Ruby, with a total of 1,800 seeds (just what the bloody hell we are going to do with the best part of 2,000 swedes I can't imagine. A lot of haggis, I guess). There is sweetcorn – F1 Sundance, which has an RHS award, although for what I do not know, and F1 Indian Summer as the catalogue said that it has 'multicoloured kernels'. Now that I have the photograph-emblazoned packet in front of me I can see what they mean; some of them look as if they are either burnt or rotten. Two types of peas, also – Onward, which I gather are pretty much ubiquitous and about the only thing that Ted and Ken seem to agree on, and Ambassador chosen for reasons known only in the ether. Possibly because we liked the shape of the word.

Looking at these paper rectangles full of DNA right now, it just seems so very unlikely that this is ever going to happen. I can only conclude that for it to be possible for us to be eating out of them in seven or eight months' time there must be some dark and disturbing forces at work. We obviously won't grow 1,800 swedes, and even if we grow only one, it will still weigh many times more than all these packets put together. And the elastic band. How is it that something as insignificant as a swede seed can grow to be something weighty enough to commit a fairly serious crime with? I know that there are all sorts of ways to explain it scientifically. There's stuff about dormancy and germination and photosynthesis, and I realize there is a process by which plants take chemicals and nutrients from the soil, which I don't know the word for. But I am glad that I do not know this word. Indeed, I am glad that I don't know much more about it than I have written here. Too much knowledge, too much analysis and too much understanding would make it so prosaic and commonplace, and I think, naïve and drippy as it may sound, that gardening should always be, in part at least, poetic and magical. Having said that, I am now going to look at the pictures in *Cassell's Encyclopaedia of Gardening* which, earlier on, was serving very well as a footstool.

5 December

I like to go to the allotment even – especially – if I have no intention of actually doing anything constructive there. I may pull up the odd weed or two on these occasions, but more as an act of territorialism than of horticulture. Often, Steve and I will come up here for no other reason than to be somewhere other than where we were. Steve and Liz live in a flat whose layout is exactly the same as mine, therefore in a physical as well as metaphorical sense, Steve and I inhabit very similar spaces. Somehow, though, however close we are in many ways, it is truly this allotment which provides us with some real common ground.

Recently, after an exhausting day spent doing some very physical voluntary work on St Catherine's Hill, I visited the plot on one of these 'for no particular reason' pretexts. Having had the plot for only three months or so, it is still possible to meet a friendly or new face, and that day I encountered one which was both. Dick, 'Or Richard' – he seemed very keen to give me the option – is the owner of the squarest and neatest-looking shed on the allotments (an accolade which is unlikely to be challenged by the motley jumble of timber that Steve and I are soon to throw up in the same name) along with equally perpendicular water butts and compost bins, the latter being the only examples I have ever seen which might be called 'clean'. As I approached, he was digging over one of his four square beds to a depth of 244 mm. I've played snooker on surfaces lumpier than those. The sides were perfectly perpendicular to the surrounding turf, and the edges of the bed were bevelled at 45 degrees. Dick seems to have the only beds on the plot, possibly the only beds of this kind in the world, with hospital corners. I was simultaneously reverent and envy-green in equal measures – I thought *I* was obsessed with straight lines and right angles, but this guy's labours made our beds look, well, unmade. He seemed a little wary of me at first, possibly because I looked as if a hedge had been dragged through me backwards, but as the conversation progressed and warmed, I realized that his reticence was born more of shyness than of suspicion. Within five minutes, I felt as though I had known him for as many weeks, and his face seemed unable to vocalize his thoughts without a smile behind his placid grey eyes, which gazed evenly at me from under a blue denim baseball hat.

Our introductory chat soon became conspiratorial. He asked me, in hushed tones and with sideways glances, whether I had yet to meet Ken. It's odd, but so far I have not encountered anybody at the plot who is able to utter the name 'Ken' without also raising a long-suffering eyebrow, or stretching a sympathetic smile, often both, but always with grudging affection. Dick's tone was further affirmation that the wrath of the Stick of Ken was our collective cross to bear. I confirmed that I had indeed felt the aura of the Great One, and we chuckled our way through the usual conversation about whether he actually ever does any gardening, because nobody seems to have seen him doing so since decimalization yet his plot appears to be relatively tidy. I thought that it might still be a little early in our friendship to mention to Dick, or Richard, our telekinesis theory, as it may have scared him off.

Dick also gave me a handy tip on growing carrots (although why he was telling me in early December is anyone's guess) but then withdrew any gravitas this may initially have carried by admitting that he'd never actually managed to grow any himself. However, the theory is that you should remove as many of the larger stones from the soil as possible prior to sowing. If they hit a stone, the young roots will simply divide, as in the cases of the side-splitting examples which appeared on *That's Life!* in the 1970s and 1980s.

Dick, or Richard, also told me that when transplanting leeks from the seed bed to the main bed (something that even the most preliminary research tells me won't be happening for at least another six months) it is good to trim both the roots and tips of the young plants before popping the leekling into the hole. You should then fill it with water as opposed to soil. Leeks need plenty of water – wonderful. I asked Dick whether he'd managed to grow any leeks himself. A question which, having not taken into account his potential sensitivity concerning carrots, sounded much more pointed than it was intended to be.

He gestured behind his right shoulder with his

thumb, which led my gaze to four militarily marching rows of prize leeks. F1 Welsh Triffid, at a guess. I asked him whether he lined the holes with compost or anything before planting. He shook his head and managed to pull down the corners of his mouth while continuing to beam with the rest of his face: 'Grow like buggery anyway – no need.'

We talked for another twenty minutes or so, during which time I complimented him sycophantically on the immaculate state of his plot (noticing also that the interior of his shed was in a similar condition), after which I made my excuses – that I am a spineless and lily-livered wimp, and a mere six hours of hacking and humping what had been gratuitously heavy and spitefully spiky bushes across uneven, rabbit-hole-infested chalky grassland and throwing them on a big bonfire, while fun in an acutely masochistic kind of way, had made me feel more strange and unbalanced than any all-night party ever had. I left, swerving and staggering, to put the car in the dog and fly home.

6 December

I had something of a seminal moment today. Perhaps 'seminal' is a bit grand. Disturbing, perhaps. Whichever, it was one of those moments when you realize that the person you thought you were is actually being someone else, somewhere else and is almost certainly having a better time doing it than you ever did. You are still not quite sure who that means you are *now*, but you have a disturbing feeling that it is someone very like your father. Half past two saw me in Hillier Garden Centre in order to look at some books and eye up what I would buy if I had the money, or steal if I hadn't been brought up a Catholic. I had left Charlie in the car – they allow dogs in there, but I suspected that the combination of bird tables *and* Christmas trees may be a urinary temptation too far, and feared that I might look down from an absorbing chapter on potato husbandry only to see Charlie standing three-legged and pissing on a bauble.

On the way in, my attention was arrested by the stack of propagators just inside the door. Of course, this was the idea – if the display had been any more obtrusive, I would have had to have picked one up and bought it simply to get in. They were only twenty quid, and I was tempted to blow the weekly food budget there and then, but I remained firm and, reducing a neat pile of propagators to a straggle of so many scattered boxes, continued my march towards the books – items which require much more resolve and far better excuses than hungry children to not buy them. For one reason or another, Steve and I haven't done much work on the plot recently, so I've been salving my conscience by reading about it instead. Or at least looking at pictures of people gardening.

Hillier's seems pretty relaxed when it comes to customers treating their bookshelves as they would a reference library – as long as you don't start eating the pages while stripping naked and barking it seems that you can browse for as long as you like. Which I did. I looked at all sorts of stuff which I had no intention of ever buying, finishing off with John Brookes's substantial, possibly even seminal, volume on garden design. It was just after replacing this on the shelf, and while I was making my way towards the Shiny and Sharp Tools section, that I had my 'disturbing' moment. I was excited. Not 'interested', 'entertained' or 'amused', but 'excited'. I was in a bloody garden centre, looking at spades and books about vegetables, and was *excited*. Not in any sexual sense, of course – John Brookes had put paid to any question of that – but as with the seeds on Sunday, it was not the excitement of actuality and realization, but of the anticipation of a myriad of possibilities. I call that disturbing. Excited. In a garden centre. Is this what my life has come to? I really need some help. And a nice cup of cocoa and a bun.

Also needing help was a middle-aged Hampshire

Lady – immaculate, three-quarter-length cashmere hairdo framing a face which had seen such an easy life that it probably assumed all ships were hard. I had forsaken the tools and thought I'd go outside for a while to price up the chicken manure pellets. As I walked through the automatic door, Celia (Arabella? Felicity? Barry?) was awkwardly semi-dragging, semi-walking a bird table towards the till. Her gyrations and puffings suggested that this was the most arduous and troublesome task she had ever had to perform. It is entirely possible that this was the truth of the matter. She and the table seemed entwined in some bizarre courtship dance, and only one of them knew the steps. Unfortunately, it wasn't her. She may have thought that she was glowing – the deferential staff may have perceived her as perspiring – but from where I was standing she really looked like she was sweating. In my excitement (yes, it was still there on the way to the chicken shit), I forgot that I am a miserable, good-for-nothing, rude, unaccommodating and belligerent loser, and offered to help. I carried her table to the till and she looked surprised, even a little begrudging, as she thanked me. I cannot help but think, having drawn no alternatives, that this was simply because she was taken aback by the fact that someone was offering to help her out on a purely altruistic basis, with no expectation of any kind of reward.

As much as she seemed surprised by, and not particularly grateful for, my assistance, I was kind of disappointed by her reaction. Until then I'd been under the impression that all gardeners were of a similar disposition – friendly, affable, egalitarian souls who understand the abstract notion of a common and collective 'good' and who do not express outright surprise and grudging gratitude when someone helps them out. I had come to think that gardening is, at least in part, about a fuller appreciation of our place in the scheme of things, and leads to some kind of inner calm and generosity of spirit. Surely, I thought, it is impossible to have a conversation about azaleas with a rude or obnoxious soul. I still refuse to believe it. Maybe she had just broken a nail.

4 Being Like Bob and Dick

Not Bob, or Dick

9 December

Sat down at my desk to write after having spent an unashamedly misty-eyed quarter of an hour or so with an arm round each of my two sons while Mum, who is visiting for a few days, made up ghoulish and bloody stories in order to ease them into an untroubled and dreamy sleep. Thought I'd better come and start writing before she finishes saying goodnight to them in case the old trout is entertaining any delusions about engaging me in meaningful conversation. You'd have thought she'd know better by now.

I was disappointed sorely today. I've heard the name Bob Flowerdew a number of times over the last few years, mainly on *Gardener's Question Time* on Radio 4. And Bob just seems like, well, such a nice bloke. And herein lies part of my problem. At first I assumed that Bob Flowerdew was to Eric Robson what Samantha is to Humphrey Lyttleton on *I'm Sorry I Haven't a Clue*, i.e. he did not exist, or his was perhaps a joke name along the lines of Hugh Jass or Tess Tickles. But he, and his name, both turned out to be real, and I resigned myself to the fact that I would never be able to lay claim to a moniker as charming, whimsical or as apposite as his.

The increase of my interest in gardening has also focused the concentration with which I listen to *GQT*, and Bob in particular, as his main area of expertise is organic fruit and vegetable growing. All his responses are delivered with the same degree of humour, assuredness and reliability as you would expect from your most trusted friend.

But it's remarkable how easily respect and admiration can be tipped over the line into irrational hatred by nothing more than jealousy. Until today, when I took

Mum to Hillier's Library, I have consoled myself with the notion that he is probably either exceptionally ugly (good face for radio) and therefore can't get sex, or very old and therefore is going to die soon. In my wildest fantasies, I imagined both to be true so that not only had he not got long left, but also was going to croak without being able to remember what it's like to get laid. Not pleasant, granted, but I've got to get through the night somehow. Well, I saw a picture of Bob on the back of a book earlier. And as well as having an amusing and appropriate name, an encyclopaedic knowledge of a subject about which I know roughly three and a half things, and a humorous, intelligent and disarming manner, he is a smashing-looking bloke to boot – waist-length plaited and shining hair, confident, beaming face, perhaps a bit older than me but an awful lot wiser. The frightening thing about this, to a hardened and con-vinced atheist such as me, is that this is possible proof that there is in fact a God, and his name's Bob.

But lifting my petty and self-absorbed mood is the fact that Mum bought me an early Christmas present, consisting of a bloody great pair of loppers complete with a free pair of hedge shears. Now I can give those buddleias out the back a really hard time. Belting. I suppose I'd better go and talk to the old trollop now.

14 December

Possibly because it is 10.40 in the evening and I have been up and about feeding, clothing and entertaining the boys since eight o'clock this morning, I felt compelled to write. The boys and I went up to the allotment this afternoon. Gabriel's idea, I think, so doubly rewarding in view of the fact that both of them have shown next to no interest in the place till now. Steve had called to see if I/we would be interested in a spot of shed preparation, but I explained that we'd already decided on digging if he fancied joining us. He didn't. Dylan, who is five and a half years old, had been persuaded to come to the plot by virtue of having been designated chief worm hunter and soil flinger. Gabriel, three and a half years older, was perhaps just curious. Maybe he's noticed that I have changed since starting on the allotment. Although what may have swayed him more was my suggestion that he straighten up the edges of their bed so that they looked like Dick's – the level of mirth engendered in a nine-year-old by this sentence should need no explanation.

Ted had beaten us to the plots. This is not entirely surprising, as by the time we arrived there was already a whisper of darkness about the day. Ted was continuing, and apparently winning, his one-man war against the roots, weeds and rocks on his plot, but still found the time to raise a salutatory fork and a toothy smile, along with his usual cheery 'Hello'. I'm constantly amazed at his jovial demeanour while hard at work. Quite often it's all I can do to whisper 'Bastard' to Steve through clenched teeth and wheezing lungs while I'm digging.

After I made sure that Dylan was quite happy getting his whole self muddy and talking (as well as listening, knowing him) to the worms, I got Gabe going by helping him to set out a line to dig along. I then tried to pass on some father–son stuff about the best way to dig and turn turf over, but soon realized that the best, and indeed only, way to dig and turn turf over is the way that feels most comfortable to you and therefore, by definition, cannot be taught. The only way for him to learn properly is the same way that everybody else does. By doing it wrong, enough different ways, long enough, for it to hurt. We learn the right way to do many things by painfully eliminating the alternatives.

'Daddy, how difficult can it be to make my edges look like Dick's?' Gabriel remained insistent that he knew perfectly well what he was doing.

Dylan was doing fantastic work on the worm front, and I laid out a plastic bag secured by two stones for him to put them on. I told him that, as a special treat, when he had collected enough worms, he could put them in the compost bin. He told me that the worms said, 'Mmmmmmmmm ... yummy compost.' In this way, Dyl gets to indulge his quite healthy and normal obsession with all things creepy/crawly/slimy/dirty/gooey, and the compost gets worms – essential to the process of breaking down the scraps – at the same time.

While Gabriel was digging along one edge, I marked out and scored the bottom edge of what is to be the potato bed. I had got about a third of the way along when he stopped and, putting his foot on his spade, looked up at me.

'I'm having a great time, Daddy!'

It is mid-December, the day was as cold and grey and uninspiring as a sweaty school sock; the drizzle, which I had optimistically predicted to lift, had that air of permanence to it as does an uninvited and tedious guest, and here was my son not only beaming, but also telling me about it, simply because he was digging. I wanted to write about this for no other reason than if I do not record these moments then they will become lost to me, and consequently to the boys. Perhaps it will also encourage a few more people to get outside with their kids and discover what fun can be had in making things look like Dick's.

5 Gone in Sixty Weeks

Killarney's Finest

17 December

Shrub, *n.* a low woody plant, a bush *esp.* one with little or no trunk.
Tree, *n.* a large plant with a single branched woody trunk.

Thus spake *Chambers Twentieth Century Dictionary* which, of course, is *the* one to have if you only have room for a small one, and utterly essential if you have any more than a passing interest in cryptic crosswords.

Not much cop, though, if you want to find out the definitive difference between a tree and a shrub. Steve and I were keen to know whether the distinction was made on the basis of size and, if so, was that in terms of height or girth? Is a tree taller than a person and a shrub shorter, and, if so, how tall is that person? Is it a child person or a grown-up person? A boy person or a girl person? A nice person or a nasty person? It was all too much for us. In desperation we thought we'd try coming at the problem from an entirely different angle. Steve was the tinderbox for this flash of divine inspiration.

'Why don't we look in the *Reader's Digest Book of Trees and Shrubs*?'

I thought maybe he was on to something. As I plucked it from beside its companion volume, the 'Reader's Digest Guide to Seeing the Wood for the Trees', I complimented him on his remarkably shrewd piece of lateral thinking.

Astonishingly, it details hundreds of different species, both large and low, all plants and all woody in one way or another, but does not see fit to offer any explanation as to the botanical difference between the two. In desperation we tried *Cassell's Encyclopaedia* – surely any book large enough to be used as occasional furniture should be able to help out. In my original, handwritten, manuscript I noted that neither book bore any fruit. I am sorry.

This kind of intensive research can be thirsty work, as can spending a couple of hours or so stripping and cleaning all the tongue and groove from the old garage doors we have salvaged in readiness for becoming a shed. So we slaked our thirsts with unmeasured beer and fingers of whisky.

Funnily enough, after a while we found ourselves not actually giving any kind of a damn what the difference between a shree and a trub was, and instead turned our attention to the more pressing matter of what we were going to plant where on the allotment. After all, we observed, there are only about a hundred days to go before we start sowing, and we don't want to get caught in the folds of the time concertina. To give ourselves a good idea of where everything was going, we laid out the seed packets in a formation similar to that of the beds on our plot. We figured that this diagrammatic representation would work better for us than drawing it out, first because a graphic image, especially a colour one, will reside in the mind's eye long after a simple annotated line diagram, and secondly because neither of us could, by that point, be trusted to hold a pencil safely. We became very fussy about the relative size of the plots, and had to fold the pea packets in half in order to achieve the correct scale. We were a bit stuck for potatoes, as we haven't got our seed yet, so we improvised with a handful of oven chips from the freezer.

We still did not know the difference between a tree and a shrub, but at least we now knew where our carrots were going to be tunnelling themselves into rude shapes this summer, and we didn't reckon that was too bad.

'Whiddowegoangethadbens?'

Steve had evidently reached that point of combined tiredness and tipsiness where he had accidentally started to say things that he thought he was just rehearsing inside his head.

'Huh?' I knew very well that I was capable of no more than one syllable at a time.

'Why. Don't. We. Go. And. Get. That. Bench?' His lips shaped the words as deliberately as if they had never tried them before. Effectively they hadn't.

Ironically, he was also sufficiently inebriated to entertain the notion that we were in a fit enough state to salvage the old picnic table which had been leaning against a local wall for over a year. It had been upended and dumped there fairly unceremoniously, and every time we walked past it we'd made a mental note that we must come and pick it up, as it did not look as if there was anything wrong with it. There wasn't when we first saw it, but it now bore the patina of four seasons' passing. That's the trouble with mental notes – they're fine, as long as you have something to make them on.

However, it was still worth rescuing. Despite my initial protestation that I was quite obviously in no fit state to walk, taking the car was not a legally or morally acceptable option. So we donned gloves, hats, coats, scarves and boots and strode off purposefully into the night – chancers, renegades, drunkards. It should really go without saying that 'strode off purposefully' should be read as 'played human pinball using the hedges, cars and each other as bumpers'.

'Where the bloody hell's it gone?'

'Bastards!'

'Who the fuck would have taken that?'

'It was a piece of crap!'

'Bastards!'

'I don't fucking believe this!'

'Someone's nicked our fucking bench!'

'Bastards!'

Stevie had seen it there only the day before, the first time I spotted it was well over two equinoxes ago and, as far as we know, nobody had touched it in between times. We walked home more amused and philosophical than angry and frustrated, and concluded that there must be an optimum time-window for salvaging urban jetsam such as this – too soon, and there is a risk that the article has only been placed there temporarily by its owner to get it out of the way. This is called stealing. But leave it too long and it will be either carted off to the tip or snapped up by someone else, and the only time you'll actually do anything about it is when you're sozzled enough to believe it's worth the effort and by then it's too late. This is called irritating. Steve and I concluded that there were too many variables (location, subjective beauty, objective and/or material value, etc.) to be able to accurately predict where the parameters of this period of time lie, but in this case the upper limit was just before we turned up.

19 December

It is only 9.25 in the morning, and already I have discovered something of curious interest. Before 10 a.m. it is usually all I can do to remember where the kettle is, but today felt different for some reason. I awoke with an inexplicable urge to trawl speculatively through the same trees and shrubs book that proved so useless on Monday night, and found myself staring at a photograph of a Killarney Strawberry Tree (Arbutus unedo), an example of which, I learned recently, sits pretty outside my back door. To my delight, I found out that the 'unedo' bit derives from the Latin 'un edo', meaning 'I eat one (only)'. This refers to the fruit of this tree, and Gabriel and I can testify to this epicurean unloveliness (Dylan was the only one of the three of us to have the sense to stick with his natural and entirely commendable response of revulsion when asked to eat anything looking like excised male genitalia). For the rest of us, learning that something may be vile but harmless to eat, can lead to only one type of research; I ate mine, I imagine, with the face of a man chewing something that looks very like a shrivelled testicle and has all the taste and texture of a wet egg box. Gabriel, I know because I saw it, looked like a nine-year-old child ejecting any and all loose contents of his mouth spontaneously, involuntarily and indiscriminately over a surprisingly wide area of the drive. 'Arbutus niledo' then, Gabe.

6 Bleak Midwinter Indeed

south of Hunter Park

13 January

Monday morning. Just spent a good part of it convincing myself that it was actually worth getting out of bed. Too often since the turn of the year I have awoken with that horribly familiar, but utterly unfounded 'just what is the point?' feeling jarring through me – as if the plunging spade of positivity has hit the subterranean rock of reality with a blunt scrape and a dull spark. Just as soon as I could pluck up the courage to do so, I peered through the spying-sliver in the shut-for-the-winter curtains. For the first morning in over a week the landscape was not dusted with frost. This meant that I could dig. Whatever else I deemed wrong with my life, I could still dig. St John's Wort? Pah! Fresh air and exercise, that's Nature's Prozac! God, I'm starting to sound like Ken.

I clambered out of bed and, before making tea, checked that there was enough electricity in the key-meter to boil the kettle. Of the 500 allocated emergency pennies 37 remained. I made a cup to drink there and then, and a flask for the rest of the day. The power will have gone off by the time I get back. As I write, I am sitting on an upturned bucket drinking a steaming lid-full of the stuff. I'd better ration it. Have I got enough petrol in the car to get to the nearest available shop – Stanmore convenience store in Winchester – to recharge the key?

I fed the dog, then myself, after which I washed the ghosts of yesterday's dinner and readied myself for a cold morning's digging. Charlie wanted to come with me, but I patiently explained that it was too cold for him and that he would be more comfortable at home. I didn't like to tell him that the real reason is that he is a right pain in the arse up here sometimes, and when I am in this sort of mood it is possible that I will kill him if he pisses on Ted's leeks or runs over everyone else's plot to greet his (imaginary) friends. Today I was too eager – I wanted to get on. I went out to the 'garden' shed to fetch my bucket containing the likely kit. I jettisoned the unnecessaries – the boys' hand-forks, the trowel, the inexplicable pieces of spare wood, and the broken tape measure which, finally realizing that without its plastic housing it was neither use nor ornament, I attempted to throw away. As I did so, it unfolded and swish-sprung out of the bin and stiffened itself into a perfectly straight yellow line on the drive, like some 15 feet long, self-inflating parking restriction. Sometimes, that feeling you get at the beginning of the day can be so terribly accurate. I picked up my fork, spade and bucket, and on the way past the front door I chucked the flask and my journal into the bucket, and made my way up here.

The soil, on first inspection, looked welcoming – all loose and crumbly. Perfect. I put down the bucket, and laid my largely ceremonial spade next to it. Choosing my spot, I rammed the fork into the soil, as if claiming it like Aldrin did the moon. But there was no scything and satisfying penetration of the soil. It wasn't rock either. Just resistance. Like picking up a box which is heavier than it looks. Awkward and off-balance. Something hurt a little somewhere unlikely. I levered and lifted what I could – a splintering scrape revealed brown clods flecked with crystal shards of spine-shivering ice. Still frozen.

I've read more than once that if the ground is frozen it should be left well alone for the frost to do its thing – breaking down the soil or something like that. Who am I to argue? So now I'm sitting on my bucket, really wondering what the point of getting up was, while Charlie sits on the sofa, wondering the same two things he always puzzles over – 'When is dinner?' and 'Who is Charlie?' Now that I'm up, and up here, the least I can do is get some of the bigger stones off the carrot patch.

At least I can say I've actually done some sort of gardening-related activity over the last week or so which is a damn sight more than Steve can. He is, as I write, cavorting around New York or New England or somewhere like that with Lizzie. However, there are benefits to be had from his sojourn. The only one that springs to mind immediately, apart from the obvious advantage of being able to go through their cupboards, is the fact that I can temporarily make decisions about the plot without having to consult him first. There is a kind of unwritten (and unspoken, come to think of it) agreement between us which requires a nod from the other when it comes to plot matters. This understanding has sprung from a deep and abiding trust, respect and love for each other. That and the fact that neither of us is capable of making sensible or safe decisions on our own. But now that he isn't here I'm quite relishing the freedom afforded by this new-found autonomy. Mainly because it means I get to choose where the shed goes. After the frost had thwarted my attempt at digging earlier, I did spend a good amount of time removing as many stones as my numb fingers could hold from the soon-to-be carrot bed (bed 'b'). I got up about half a bucket-load and dumped them next to where the shed is going to be whether Christopher effing Columbus likes it or not. We were initially going to put it on the plot itself, where the old corrugated compost bin was until I took it to the tip, but I figured that it would be better at the top of the plot (to the south of the potato bed) for two reasons. First, it will be more sheltered from the elements there; between it and the prevailing winds will be two decent-sized shrubs, or possibly trees (one of which I may have killed the other day by 'pruning' it). Because of the homespun nature of the shed, I feel that it may need more help than most against the lashings it will receive from both rain and wind. I have horrible images of the whole thing being picked up and ignominiously plonked on someone's prize Brussels sprouts, so have every intention of bracing it in every way imaginable. I reckon that this natural barrier will aid the process.

The second reason for putting the shed here is far more critical. This site is marginally higher than the other, and consequently has a better view of the gate on the far side of the allotments. This means that we will be able to spot Ken coming sooner, and will therefore have a few more precious seconds in which to hide all our tools, muzzle our dogs and cower inside the shed. The ability to hide from the rest of the world is one of the main reasons for building a shed in the first place, so making surveillance and early warning two of our top priorities seems eminently sensible.

I figure that with the tongue and groove we've already got, we can cover about 40 square feet of walls. The remainder can be clad with the overlap stuff from the fence panels in my garden which I'm going to strip some time this week. Not ideal, but free, and considering that we're taking what's left of the ten-pound shed budget to the pub when it is up, it'll have to do. The revised target – having not even narrowly missed our Christmas deadline – is to get the shed up by the end of this month. Steve is due back in a week or so, and then has a huge number of shifts to do in order to pay for his holiday, but we should be able to get building soon after that.

14 January

It is said that nature abhors a garden. Well she cannot conceivably have more loathing for mine than I do right now. I know that I have no one but myself to blame (Culpability Brown – guilty as charged) for the fact that it cannot currently be described without a parenthesising pair of inverted commas. It comprises an L-shaped area of ground, with maximum dimensions of approximately 30 feet by 40 feet. The tenants who occupied the flat before me evidently knew roughly the same amount about gardening as I do – perhaps a bit less. There are two areas of concrete – one square, one rectangular – with the remainder of the 'garden' laid to weeds. About ten months ago I made a feeble attempt to tidy it up a bit – the gardening equivalent of preparing a ready-meal. I now realize that waving an old billhook at a patch of weeds does not constitute gardening any more than heating up a plastic tray of anonymous slop constitutes cooking. Unfortunately, the weeds I slashed were predominantly brambles and bindweed, which apparently thrive on this sort of treatment, and they have now all but taken over.

Today I have removed the two fence panels which partially divided one area from the other – mainly because I wanted to open the 'garden' out, but also because we need the panelling for our shed. Where the panels were, there were also some daunting-looking reed-type things – no idea what they were, and quite frankly I don't care because I don't like them anyway (or at least I didn't like them until I dug them up). Now I detest them. Surely such spindly, ungainly, stork-legged stems don't need such huge, ugly, gnarly roots. Maybe, in terms of natural selection, that's all they've got going for them. They don't look pretty, I very much doubt you can eat them, and not even I am going to try to smoke them, so it stands to reason that people keep them only because it's too much bloody effort to do anything else. Not for me it's not. I laid into them with my spade in a noisy, violent and sweaty outburst (think somewhere between Jack Nicholson and Monty Don) before levering out the severed segments with the fork and heaving them onto the Garden Waste pile.

There are two main piles in the 'garden'. There are, of course, sub-piles, but the two main ones are the Garden Waste pile, which is actually rather small in comparison to the other one – the Bonfire pile. Which is also known as the 'garden'. As if these gnarled behemoths were not enough, a previous resident of this place had obviously seen fit to provide what I am sure is more than adequate drainage to the soil by the addition of a generous quantity of half-bricks and fist-sized lumps of concrete, resulting in more of those bone-jarring shocks every so often when plunging into the soil.

Premature arthritis and/or osteoporosis? Consistent backache? Permanently lacerated forearms? Bits of God-knows-what flicking into the eyes? Ah! The pacific joys of this tranquil pursuit of gardening! Strange thing is, though, and this is true of nearly every gardening day which has started with a bleak, uphill morning recently, I still feel quantifiably and remarkably better than I did when I woke up. Mother Nature may well abhor a garden, but Father Time, it seems, can make us somewhat partial to them.

7 Mendel's Maracas

5,423

15 January

Today is sweetcorn day. Not in any culinary sense, but because it is the day that I have chosen to trawl through my textbooks and fill in my sweetcorn 'veg fact sheet'. Both of our chosen varieties are, I am assured by my most reliable of growing guides (i.e. their packets), F1 hybrids. Out of interest I looked this up in order to find out exactly what an F1 Hybrid actually is, but a combination of poor archiving (why didn't I write it down?) and amnesia (why didn't I write it down?) means that I could remember neither the answer to this question, nor its source. I scoured my growing collection of 'vegetable gardening for morons' books to no avail before inspiration struck – I knew that the dog-eared biology textbook I rescued from the tip last year sometime 'because it would come in handy one day' would come in handy one day.

Monohybrid inheritance (Mendel's Law of Segregation)

Monohybrid inheritance refers to the inheritance of a single character only. One trait which Mendel studied was the shape of the seed produced by his pea plants. This showed two contrasting forms – round and wrinkled. When he crossed plants which were pure breeding for round seed with ones pure breeding for wrinkled seed, all the resulting plants produced round seed. The first generation of a cross is referred to as the **first filial generation (F1).**[1]

Interesting guy, I'm sure, but I thought that wrinkly peas were the ones that had dried out and were only of any further use in the domestic manufacture of 'musical' instruments for small children. Mendel may never have had children, choosing instead material prosperity, a

1 *Understanding Biology For Advanced Level*, Glenn and Susan Toole, 1995 ed, Stanley Thornes (Publishers) Ltd, Cheltenham (ISBN 0 74871718 8).

clear head and a worthwhile career when young enough to appreciate it, but if he did – and it is to be hoped that he did, considering the line of work he was in, even if only so he could count them – they were obviously deprived the pleasures of homespun percussion, because evidently their dad was ruthlessly intent on counting peas, as the book, quite delightfully, elucidates:

> When individuals of the F1 generation were intercrossed the resulting **second filial generation (F2)** produced 7,324 seeds, 5,474 of which were round and 1,850 wrinkled. This is a ratio of 2.96:1.[2]

Now I'm as pedantic as the next man (and quite a lot more pedantic than the one next to him), but could we not have made do with 3:1?

All this, though, raises two points. First, if Mendel *did* have children, what was the reaction to the following hypothetical exchange in his study?

Mendel Five thousand four hundred and twenty-two, five thousand four hundred and twenty-thr—

Mendel Jr Dad, can I have some of those wrinkly peas so I can make some maracas?

Secondly, it's 2.958918919:1. If a job's worth doing, then it's worth doing properly, as my uber-pedant of a father used to say.

2 Ibid.

8 Digging for Sympathy

Ted – Proper Job

23 January

I came up here to level the designated (by me) spot for
our shed to sit on, optimistically armed with two garden
lines, one of the bent forks and a spade, along with my
journal and the compulsory flask. The fact that the shed
base is of certain dimensions, and needs to be placed on
a level site does not seem to have prompted me into
bringing either a tape measure or a spirit level. I became

aware of these omissions not long after leaving the house, but reckoned that my boot would serve as the former (I like to call my boot a foot) and that if I haven't got a good enough eye to tell whether a 7 feet by 5 feet bit of ground is level or not, then I shouldn't be building on it in the first place. However, it transpires that I'm going to need my secateurs and my loppers to get rid of some of the more vicious greenery in order to get at where I want to dig, so I may as well get the aforementioned tools as well.

And a rake.

And a plank to sit the spirit level on.

Might as well top the flask up while I'm there too.

27 January

I remembered all of it! Granted, this was only because I had written it down, so I can't claim to be memory man or anything, but still remarkably good, considering I don't always remember to look at reminders. There is now a beautifully level 8 feet by 6 feet rectangle sliced into the slight incline at the top of the plot. It turns out that my boot, quite poetically, is just over a foot. I found this out when I measured it accurately yesterday, having forgotten to take the tape measure a second time on Thursday. Okay, so I remembered *nearly* all of it, but hey, I'm a busy man with a lot on my mind. That, or I'm a lackadaisical and vacuous numbskull. Either way, the patch of earth I have quite civilly engineered is big enough and level enough for our shed to sit on and that is all I care about.

Since then, I have continued to remove as many large stones from the beds as I can (especially the one which is to host the carrots), and to chuck them onto this flat, level but squishy surface in order to compact and firm it before we put the shed on it. This all seems to fit together nicely – we need to get some of the stones out, otherwise the vegetables will get at best confused and at worst stubborn, while at the same time the shed needs a nice firm base. A perfectly symbiotic relationship between the yin and yang, the hard and the soft. We remove some rocks from the land in order to support the shed, which will in turn house the tools with which we will work the land. Symbiotic balls, more like. I must never lose sight of the fact that I am digging soil and putting up a shed, otherwise my head will disappear so far up my own backside that it might just end up between my shoulders again, which would not be a pretty sight.

Where was I? Oh yes; the next day found me back at the plot in speculative mood. It was all looking a bit, well, neglected and sorry for itself – like the old bloke at the Christmas party who nobody seems to know and who has fallen asleep, torn paper hat askew and plastic Kazoo dribbling from the corner of his mouth. For me, Christmas usually serves only, and very temporarily, to alleviate the long, grey haul through winter, and the trouble is that everything just looks so much more ostentatiously drab and bare once the tinsel's down. Kind of naked and uncomfortable. We didn't put any paper chains up at the plot but it still managed to look mighty pissed off anyhow. The potato bed, along with the one that we have finally decided is to be the carrot and onion patch (the scent of the onions deters the carrot root fly), was still covered with old bits of half-made compost and rather forlorn-looking leaves which can't even be bothered to rot properly. The rest of the beds were tending towards plain slovenliness, as if they had put on a few pounds over the break. They also had more than a few green tufts of various types of weeds and grasses, no doubt with disproportionately long, complicated and brittle root systems.

I decided to rectify this situation, Steve or no Steve, and do the First Bit of Digging of the Year. Levelling the bank for the shed didn't count, as this was a shed-centred as opposed to a veg-centred activity, and therefore one which fell resoundingly under the 'displacement' category. For digging to be real digging, you must have asked yourself at least two of the following questions: 1) Why did I start doing this? 2) Will I ever finish doing this? 3) Is it still acceptable to cry through pain in public? Or 4) Will I always walk like this? Bearing this in mind, I weighed up the options for which patch to start with, considering all sorts of different criteria; which one is to be planted first, which would benefit most from my attentions, which would yield the most satisfaction, etc. Eventually I plumped for the only sensible option – the smallest one with the least amount of matted, not-quite-rotten-enough inverted flaps of turf on it. Simple really. The boys' plot it was, then. However much I knew that I should make a start on the 450 square foot monster of a potato bed we have lumbered ourselves with, I also knew that today was less about tentatively 'making a start' than resound-ingly reaching a conclusion. For some reason it struck me that the First Bit of Digging of the Year should be something which you finish the same day you start it. A plump, lumpy brown rectangle of soil, aerated and risen like a good loaf just looks as if somebody *gives* a damn about the place. I figured that it might even make me feel like *I* gave a damn about the place. It worked. I did (finish it), it did (look like somebody gave a damn), and I did (give a damn). If I say so myself, I didn't do a bad job either. In fact, it was Ted who said exactly that the day after I'd managed to walk again. He should know. He's seventy-four and probably been digging for longer than I've been farting or breathing, possibly both put together.

I managed to dig out most of the bits that were even vaguely green – it's coming up to that time for every-thing (except our vegetables, obviously) to start growing very rapidly indeed, and I'd rather the weeds did it somewhere other than where I intend to educate my boys in the ancient arts of pea persuasion and carrot nadgering. I broke all the soil down, removing the larger stones but leaving the smaller ones for drainage because, apparently, clay-ish soil (like ours) is less likely to bake rock-hard in the summer if it's got a few stones in the mix. I'm not going to argue. I never argue with theories that sound good, however speciously, especially when they mean less scrabbling around in the soil making your burning-cold fingers bleed. The boys' plot now actually looks as if something might grow on it – some-thing useful and possibly even edible, as opposed to the weeds I have hoiked out, which would probably grow on the moon if they had to.

I surveyed what I had achieved, after the now obliga-tory walk round the park with Charlie. This was as much an opportunity to refresh the eyes as it was to stretch the back. A break allows the eyes to see a job in its entirety, and, moreover, as a separate entity from the grubby, sweaty and sometimes tedious intermediate stages which created it. Something happens in the mind's eye. All the associations – positive and negative – which accrue during any process – pride, anger, frustration, loathing, loving and sometimes even liking – colour the receptors, the cones and rods of the inner eye, in different, sometimes conflicting ways. After a period of time away, detached, distracted and objective, all these associations, these pieces of visual baggage, if not shrugged off altogether, at least seem a little lighter.

That bed's pretty much done, then, apart from the liberal application of some of the soil conditioner that Steve bought from the tip before he left, in a pre-emptive but futile attempt to assuage his guilt. Not a bad start, and in order to continue the year on this positive note I found myself up at the allotment again yesterday.

I say 'found myself up there' as I didn't actually intend to do any digging at all, and had promised myself that I would instead spend the day copying some stuff up from my journals. But I was cajoled into gardening by a combination of auto-ennui, the weather (cold, blue sunshine) and Ted, who has made me feel guilty by toiling over his slate-flat, fine-tilthed plot equally happily day or night, sun, rain or snow. I had been walking Charlie, and was looking forward to getting home and putting the kettle on. But as I was walking past the plots, I realized that there were still a couple of hours of useful daylight left, and if I didn't take this opportunity then it would be another wasted. What's more, I'd never hear the last of it from Ted, who had spied me and waved while I was on the other side of the park. I shuffled over to the plot as enthusiastically as an errant child dawdling across the playground to an expectant and reproachful headmaster. Ted was there with his deputy and son-in-law, Roger, and their mission was to erect a fence at the top of Ted's plot in an attempt to keep wayward dogs off it. The fence consists, from what I could gather, of plain mesh topped with coiled razor wire and sharpened steel spikes smeared with the dermal excretions of 500 poison-arrow frogs (available at the local deli). In addition to this were two remotely operated CCTV cameras wired to a pair of infrared-triggered sub-machine guns.

Reluctantly, I started to dig the BIG potato patch. Mostly in order to raise a moral ground just high enough to preach from, in preparation for Steve's imminent return to the plot. I had nearly managed to dig a row and was approaching the bits of turf we had turned over at the bottom of the bed, at the same time as I saw my boredom threshold looming ominously on the horizon. At this point Roger walked past, and interrupted his whistling to comment that I must be a glutton for punishment, what with the soil being so wet. I needed no further encouragement than this to immediately cease my activities. I would hate to appear a fool, especially in front of the best gardener in Twyford.

Today, though, I thought I might have the energy to give it another go. The bed in question, at the south end of the allotment, has now been more accurately measured at 28 feet by 16 feet, including its somewhat bizarre and uneven division into two separate beds by a path of turf. I don't yet know who tended our plot before us, but I should probably find out, if not for the sake of scholarly research, then at least so I can ask them what it is that makes someone leave a strip of grass 2 feet into a veg plot. I had removed most of these inverted swards yesterday before I started my abortive digging attempt. After we had eventually decided to remove this path, it had taken Steve and me hours to dig up and turn over not only these bits of turf, but also all those necessary to square up the other beds. We had been assured more than once that this was okay, as the grasses would die and rot in situ, nourishing the soil in the process. What everyone omitted to tell us, and we were too lazy or too stupid or both to figure out for ourselves, was that this theory works in practice only if you bury the turf under at least a spade's depth of soil, as opposed to the thickness of a cigarette paper that Steve and I had deemed to be sufficient. We had 'tidied up' the bottom of this plot at the end of last year by doing just this, and today I wanted to heave these grass doormats onto the bank next to the shed plateau, along with all the others we have shifted so far. Doing this, I thought, would be a great psychological boost, as it would at least injure, if not break, the back of this seemingly monstrous tract of land. Considering the state of my tender, throbbing lumbar region now, I have an awful feeling that this may not be the only back that has been damaged today.

I got to the plot at about midday, and left just as it was getting dark. At this time of year this means about five hours of digging, which probably equates to nearer four, counting tea, chatting and sobbing breaks. Four solid, sodding hours of digging. Four hours of breaking every single Health and Safety Executive spade-work guideline (and probably some EU ones as well). Four hours of doing the same thing over and over again, all the time feeling as if it is never, ever going to end and, like school food, that it will never get any smaller or more palatable, no matter how much fork-work you put into it. However, despite all this effort and indeed pain,

I can now report that the plot is dug. Well, nearly. When I say 'nearly', I mean that there's still about a third of it to do. Quite – did I dig in slow motion today? Did I spend longer than I thought taking photographs of Ted digging? Had Ken induced some kind of mind time warp in me during what struck me at the time as an unusually brief conversation, but which actually lasted the usual three-quarters of an hour? No idea, but it felt like I was working really, really hard. I'm not sure what the going average is for four hours' digging, but right now, 300 square feet feels like a little bit more than just enough, because the only reason that I have written this much tonight is that I cannot get out of my chair.

28 January

I just don't learn, do I? Yesterday I must have made at least three references to how much I hurt after digging for so long. And did I bloody whinge about it? Of course I did – it really, really hurt. OOwwWWW! See, there I go again; I have little pride or dignity. I am a wuss. But did it stop me from going out there and doing it all over again today? Did it arse. I'm bloody Super-man, me, aren't I? I can dig all day, have a bath and a good night's sleep and do it all again without even a twinge, just like I could when I was nineteen, can't I? *Can't* I? Well, no, I can't. Well I can, but not without going 'Ooooowwwwwwwww! Bloody buggering ooooooowwwwwwww bollocks owwwwwwwwwww' whenever I breathe in or move my little finger. Every time I close my eyes (which is frequently) all I see is a tangled, seething mass of straggly weeds and couch grass roots. The arterial squiggles of their roots are now imprinted on my retina (or is it simply that I can see my own straining blood vessels)?

Did I mention dandelion roots? Must have pulled twenty today if I pulled one. What I don't understand about dandelion roots is why they are so bloody big in comparison with their leaves. I mean, it's not as if they are especially tall, but they obviously think that it's necessary to have huge, often forked, tap roots reaching down seemingly into middle earth. There is, however, an upside to this. Instead of petulantly discarding these roots, exact proper revenge by cleaning them off well and drying them thoroughly in a warm oven until they are brittle to the core. Then grind the little bastards up and pour boiling water over them. Kind of like coffee from a muddy cup, but not bad. And the very young, very pale leaves can be used in a mixed green salad if there's no hemlock, but avoid the dark green, tougher leaves at all costs because they taste like what I would imagine to be the result of combining wasabi and cheap instant coffee.

I couldn't have wriggled out of digging today if I'd tried, mainly because after yesterday I couldn't wriggle my way out of a seed packet. Steve has been working since he got back, and when we spoke I promised him that we would dig today if the weather was fine. The poor bloke's done so little recently that to him digging is once again such a novelty that he still gets excited about it. Bless him. Lazy sod.

We set ourselves the task of finishing off the potato bed, and started by removing the turf that I missed on Sunday – one of the things I've learned about digging is that success is predominantly to do with rhythm; if the soil is decent and there are not too many large rocks to jangle your bones on, then you soon find a pace and a tempo which suits you. Having to stop at the end of each row to clear these grassy lumps breaks this rhythm. I guess that it could be argued that varying the type of activity you are doing helps to stretch and contract different muscles but never mind all that – we actually *want* to hurt and bleed and get dirty in the process. Most blokes do. Anyway, the rhythm of digging can get kind of hypnotic and even meditative at times. Once your eyes are tuned, you get to be able to see an awful lot in a clump of soil.

Two long and agonizing hours later, we proudly surveyed our newly claimed, purposeful-looking potato bed. Less weeds, more soil conditioner and mouldy old leaves. Much less will to refuse disconcertingly expensive Belgian lager. If the plot hadn't been so dull and earthy, it would have shone like a soldier's shoe. We emptied the last bucket-load of weeds onto the bank and stones onto the shed plateau and, arching our backs and holding our hips like expectant mothers, pronounced it ready. Which reminded us that we still hadn't bought any seed potatoes.

Despite our exhaustion, we bounced home full of the energy of achievement. To an outsider it probably didn't amount to much, but we sensed that we had done something important – we had made ground ready for growing. The sound of fifteen thousand years of agricultural evolution produces deep and resonant echoes.

That afternoon, Steve and I attempted an erection together in my driveway and made many other puerile references to the prickly subject of exactly how we were going to build our shed in a manner liable to give it a fighting chance of standing upright for longer than ten minutes. It has been some weeks since we made the base and knocked the framework together (to 'flat-pack' stage) and, since then, we have been aching to temporarily wedge these sections together to give us an idea of the dimensions, constructional logistics, etc. We actually wanted to do it because we wanted to have a shed RIGHT NOW! Later, though, we felt more justified in our impetuousness, as the process was actually quite informative, and we managed to work out a specific sequence of holding, drilling, hammering and swearing in order to get it to stay up. As soon as we got this wired, we made our skeleton shed, drawn in the air with wood. It looked like it might actually work! We had to get Lizzie. Today, not only had we cultivated land ready for our fertile seed, but had also made shelter. Woman come, see man make shed. We dragged our knuckles round to Steve's place and when the three of us got back Lizzie stood 'in' the 'shed' with Steve, who picked ticks from her hair and grunted. It was so romantic. As Liz and Steve 'exited' the 'shed' (i.e. stepped off its base) the sides kind of stopped working, went all Buster Keaton, and described a graceful and accelerating arc on their way to the gravel. To use a more technical term, they fell over. There is photo-graphic evidence of Liz and Steve 'in' the 'shed'. Unfor-tunately I didn't manage to get a shot of it falling over, as I was too busy trying to catch one of the sides as it whistled towards the ground.

Right, that's it. I'm knackered. I need a bath.

9 Greenhouse Envy

Here's One I Made Earlier

3 February

The other day I spent a little longer than may be considered healthy trying to find the first reference to allotments in my diaries and journals from last year. Probably due to my insatiable desire for pedantry and detail, it somehow seemed important to know exactly when I first developed an interest in this insanity. The first reference I came across was under 13 May, which reads 'Call re: allotments'. The other three entries for that day are all 'call re:' something or other as well, and in view of the fact that one of those was 'call re: water meter' – a device which was installed only a fortnight ago – it appears that I was pretty quick on the uptake as far as the plot goes. Assuming I made the call, that is.

Whenever it was I did do so, the phone was answered by the previously mentioned Mrs Pottinger, whom I subsequently met at the allotments to negotiate our plot. So it was with some sadness yesterday that I learned she had died last week. I did not, obviously, know her well, but she seemed to be a sprightly, perceptive and engaging lady, and apparently remained that way until her last day, at the end of which she retired to bed as usual and simply did not wake up again. I am sure that, were we all given the choice, a full and active life consummated by a swift and painless death, free of the spiral of deterioration and its concomitant loss of dignity and independence, would be the option of an overwhelming majority, and I trust that this will be of some consolation to those who knew her. It is difficult to know what else to say on the subject without sounding mawkish, so I won't. Except that I do feel, since our plot may well be the last one with which she dealt, any failure on our part to grow vegetables on it will not only spell personal disaster for us, but could also be construed as being plain disrespectful. So, Pat, these spuds are for you, old girl.

This piece of news was passed on to me by another lady whose name I would not dare invent. I met Angela Forder-Stent by chance while at the park with the boys. We had gone there initially, and rather optimistically considering the stubbornness of the drizzle – at their request – to dig. In view of the relatively warm, dry alternatives I have to say that I found this show of interest in the allotment on their part not only vaguely surprising, but also immensely rewarding. That they have started to share my enthusiasm for the plot means a lot, and the fact that the majority of their time spent there consists of worm hunting and mud wrestling is irrelevant; rather that than them being stuck in front of a Gamecube all day.

However, despite this mutual desire for paternal and filial bonding, we were thwarted by wetness. The soil resembled a half-cooked and poorly mixed chocolate cake, with gravel. We tried to pull a few weeds out of their bed but it was futile – when the soil's that wet, it's all you can do to get the stuff off the roots, never mind then removing it from your fingers. This would only put them both off gardening for ever. So, surprisingly reluctantly on the boys' part, and suspiciously willingly on mine, we called it a very short day as far as digging was concerned, and instead did what all boys do when faced with such adversity. We turned our attentions to making a rope swing. This one was to be fashioned from the yellow nylon tow rope in the boot of the car and a stick roughly the size that you might throw for a strong, medium-sized dog. The boys went off to throw the latter for our medium-sized dog to chase while I retrieved the rope. As I was doing so, I noticed a well-dressed, well-coiffed and generally immaculately-turned-out lady standing at the top of our plot, apparently surveying the allotments. She had that glow of well-looked-after-ness which can only be a product of having never bought anything with a blue and white striped packet from Tesco's. As well as being in possession of the most suspiciously clean shoes on a muddy allotment I think I have ever seen, she had a clipboard. A *clipboard*. She even looked as if she knew how to operate it without hurting her fingers (unbroken, polished nails, no bruising). Anyone standing at the top of our plot with a clipboard also has one of two things: either a court order or valuable information. Either way, I had to speak to her, but a combination of nebulous guilt, inverted snobbery and traditional trepidation made me hesitate. What to say? How to break the ice with this cashmere-sweatered, pearl-earring'd, silk-scarved paragon of received pronunciation?

'What the bloody hell d'you think you're doing?'

No. Too brusque. Impolite even. Best not to cause any more alarm than my tired, grubby and unshaven state was already bound to. This time I spoke out loud.

'Do you have an allotment?'

Bugger – with the unintentional emphasis on the word 'have', this sounded like a thinly veiled euphemism for 'What the bloody hell d'you think you're doing?' It was also a bit of a stupid question to be asking someone with shoes that clean and manicured hands holding a clipboard. A bit like asking Steve if he has a clue about digging, but it was all I could think of.

She turned with a disarming smile and the reply that no, she did not, but had taken over from the parish councillor who used to look after them. It was then that she told me about Mrs Pottinger, and that she was here to figure out who had which plot – a process with which I was glad to assist as far as I could, hoping that in return she might show me what was on her clipboard.

I noted, with a degree of amusement, that her facial muscles twitched with a grimace of sympathy, affection and concern similar to everybody else's at the mention of Ken. Mrs. Forder-Stent turned out to be genuinely pleasant and very forthcoming. On her clipboard was a document which I had been seeking for some time:

a plan of the allotments – all named, numbered and, crucially, measured. I'd had visions of having to mince up and down the plots, one boot in front of the other, in order to get these dimensions for my allotment diagram, but here they were, measured in square rods (whatever they are).

I don't remember much about the rest of the conversation, as I was too busy trying to work out how I could get hold of this piece of paper without her noticing. 'Hey! Look at that big thing over there!' Point, whoosh! Gone. Even more bizarre potential methods of distraction flashed into my mind – inappropriate sexual advance? Er, no. Light but smarting jab on the nose? Perhaps not. Diplomacy, once again, must prevail, so we continued the allotment gossip. The plot immediately to the north-east of ours is, apparently, being hotly contested at the moment. I had heard mention of this the other day from Ted, who gives roughly the same amount of damns about what everyone else is up to as I do, so I was not in possession of the full details. It turns out that the supposed incumbents, having done not a stroke on the plot since pulling up a few carrots before buggering off last August, have been unwittingly usurped by some parvenus who have changed the padlock on the shed in an act of gauntlet throwing bordering on warmongering. This dispute is to be resolved next week in the parish hall by a combination of badger-wrestling, bare-knuckle-fighting and tobacco-spitting competitions. Mrs Forder-Stent sold me a ticket. I continued to nod and smile politely as if I was interested more in allotment disputes than in her piece of paper. Finally I could bear it no longer. In my most measured and articulate voice I asked her if there was any chance I could procure a copy of her plan. Not only did she agree, she also offered me access to Mrs Pottinger's records which are, she said, meticulous in the extreme. She asked that I give her a couple of months or so to allow her to access and rationalize the records in a respectful and sensitive manner. Naturally I resisted the temptation to reply that this wasn't actually that convenient, and I would appreciate it if she could hurry things along a little, but if not then it would have to do. Instead, as we parted company and as I began to stroll back to my very bored, but very patient, boys, I thanked her for her generosity in terms of her time and assistance.

The boys and I wandered around the park for half an hour or so, testing various trees in order to find one from which we could suspend our rope swing. There are two very stately and imposing examples near the tennis courts, which no doubt will serve as an idyllic backdrop to the coming summer's cricket and its crustless cucumber sandwiches, but they turned out to be crap for rope swings. Limes, I think. Or elms. Steve says oak, but then Steve points at all trees and says 'Oak!' in the same way that most men point at Kylie Minogue and say 'Bottom!' We'll have to wait for the summer and see what shape the leaves are. Whatever they are, they turned out to be lousy for our purposes, so we ended up back at the tree which we first thought might do the job, which turned out to be okay, but hardly Arthur Ransome. We concluded that the park, despite the fact that it has become a place of which we are all extremely fond, is useless in the rope-swing department. This is obviously why the local council had seen fit to put four perfectly good prefabricated swings not 25 yards from where we were standing.

Despite the obvious merits of these swings (primarily that they perform their eponymous task) the boys insisted on staying on the rope 'swing' (a more appropriate name may have been 'twirl'), possibly in deference to my fragile sensibilities more than out of any sense of enjoyment. Still I glowed with fatherly pride – if I wasn't going to show my kids how to manipulate nature to our advantage one way – by digging – then I was going to do it in another – by swinging. How very Sixties. Man come. Man make swing. Man proud.

Eventually, however, Gabriel's desire to actually swing

like a pendulum rather than dangle and spin like a builder's plumb bob overcame that which sought to flatter, and he came to sit on the swing next to me, from where I had been watching the pair of them. As we swung, trying to keep in time with each other, we watched Dylan, still happily whirling round and round in the world to which only he will ever go. Head back, dimpled hands grasping the yellow rope, eyes lightly closed and legs stretched out to intuitively provide a counterbalance. Grinning. Humming. Oblivious.

Man come. Man raise sons. Man beat chest. Man fall off swing.

After this, we played a game of 'Hide the Stick in the Sandpit'. Times are financially laughable right now, so thankfully – and probably consequentially – I have two imaginative, resourceful and easily pleased children. Therefore quaint, Dickensian games such as these happen with a regularity which might bother me were I more materialistic, but as it is I wouldn't swap my two children's imagination, resourcefulness and placability for all the material goods in the world; nor for all the money spent each year to get those goods fixed or replaced.

In the end we couldn't work out who won 'Hide the Stick in the Sandpit', mainly because in the beginning we had not discussed any rules, but also because eventually none of us could remember where the stick was anyway. I sensed that it didn't really matter, though – much as it had not mattered that our rope swing hadn't swung, or that our plot hadn't got dug. What was vitally important in each instance was that we had played the game. As we lolloped back to the car, the first few heavy drops of rain plopped onto our heads and onto the grass in front of us, bending back the blades. I reflected on the afternoon, and on the notion that our desire to make a swing, in the face of the existing ones, was born of the same impulse to grow vegetables in the full knowledge of how cheaply and easily they can be bought at any supermarket. It is not the tug of some perverse and anachronistic sense of 'Britishness', nor is it simple bloody-mindedness, which drives all but the most urbane of people to do these sorts of things. It runs deeper – it is a regression to a more natural, if a more brutal, state of being. The impulse which drives me to dig until my back creaks in order that I can grow some peas is also responsible for my making a swing. Or a shed. Or dinner. Or love. It gives rise to the satisfaction of hammering a nail in straight and true, as well as that of rocking a teething child to sleep. It is nothing less than the organic swell of being fit for our purpose, and of successfully propagating and nurturing our species.

And you can't buy that in Tesco's, no matter how fancy the packaging.

4 February

A number of things happened today which were of sufficient interest to make me think 'must write about this later'. A sign of a productive and busy day, perhaps, but unfortunately I can remember only about a third of them.

I woke up to a light dusting of frost, which dulled the hues outside as if the colour-control knob on an old television had been tweaked a few degrees anti-clock-wise. It also took some time, and three mugs of tea, to get myself properly tuned in. Digging was off the agenda due to the cold hardness of the ground, so I decided that a spot of dog walking would fully clear my morning head just as well. Just as I was creasing my trousers before placing my right foot – always the right first – into the cold abyss of my wellington boot, the phone rang (or rather it chirped shrilly in the way that only a telephone that cost five pounds can). It was Steve, asking if it would be okay if I went with him to Sparsholt College, as he was not quite sure of the way. He also needed some moral support, as he was about to hand over £235 in hard-earned and hard-saved cash for his chainsaw course in May. Because I am on state benefits, I get my courses free, so we decided to both become lumberjacks – if we can't *grow* big plants, we're going to do the next best thing and learn how to cut the buggers down. Steve also suggested that we take in a garden centre or two afterwards. Sparsholt was first, though, because if he did not pay his fees this morning he'd miss his place on the course, his world would explode, and its flying shrapnel would shatter all of his dreams. This sounds flippant, but truly, this is more than a chainsaw course for Steve; it is the inception of, and the first real commitment to, not only a change of career, but also a shift in lifestyle and outlook. You don't say 'no' to someone on that kind of mission, so I donned the five layers of clothing necessary to avoid frostbite on a motorbike in this weather and waddled next door.

At 10.15 a.m. we were thrumming around some mellow country lanes on Steve's Yamaha XS1100, with an imperious view over the lower walls and hedges not afforded by most cars. It is a cliché, but 'crisp' is by far the most appropriate word to describe the morning, in the same way that certain sunsets can only be 'Turner-esque'. The low shafts of sunlight beamed through the gaps between the flanking trees in an irregular, staccato rhythm, and refracted through our visors as we snaked along. The air was crystal cold, the light strong and yellow-white. I felt, not for the first time since we took on the allotment, as if I actually belonged within a landscape, and desired to remain a part of it. Between the ages of nineteen and thirty-two I moved house over twenty times. There is much to be said for putting down some roots. Not a great deal flowers without them.

We arrived at Sparsholt College very much awake and looking permanently surprised. It could have been the lingering effects of the cold, but I'm sure I saw a tear in Steve's eye as he parted with nearly a quarter of a thousand pounds, as I sensitively put it later. Steve's ability to save money is one which I have always both admired and coveted. His method involves a few envelopes, some will power and, every time he removes even one note from any envelope, being given a thorough grilling by Lizzie as to its provenance, destination and date of return. I have tried to emulate this method, but have failed to do so not only because I see little sense in trying to save money when sometimes I struggle to cover the phone bill, but also, in no small part, because I have no one to tell me that running low on beer is insufficient justification to raid the 'emergency' envelope. Still, it seems to do the trick for Steve, as the thirteen notes he handed over today are testament to.

He is one of my very best friends for a number of reasons. Near the top of the list is that he invariably has the capacity to restore my faith in the human race whenever my view of it gets jaded. He does this by being, quite simply, one of the most compassionate and sensitive people I have had the privilege to meet. Steve hates the idea that he may have upset someone in any way – a fact which made watching him grovel to Bernadette in registry an entertaining lesson in schaden-freude. Apparently he had had a tantrum on the phone earlier on, mainly, I suspect, due to the impending loss of 23,500 pence, and had slammed the phone down in frustration. He was at pains to point out that he was most terribly sorry, had not meant to cause any offence and were there any birch twigs available with which he could beat himself? Bernadette looked a little surprised and said that yes, it *was* she to whom he had spoken and no, she had not sensed that he had been rude and, in point of fact, remembered thinking how polite and patient he had been. Steve struggled to support and straighten his rapidly falling crest, which can't have been easy with all those jumpers on.

'Look, woman, I was pissing well rude, all right!' would have made a brilliant line, but did he use it? Did he hell. Instead he bowed and scraped his way out of the door, muttering about being British or the weather or some such twaddle. I followed behind him, wringing my hands and apologizing to Bernadette for the sorry state of Steve's apology.

Next stop was Hillier's for a browse, on the premise that the more we can soak up about all things gardening, from whatever source, the better. And if that means that we also get the vicarious pleasure of looking at shiny new books and rust-free tools and the chance to grab a coffee at the same time, then so much the better. As we wandered about, it struck me that it is really not long now before everything starts going 'bang!' in an wild orgy of fecundity. For the first time I realized that spring does not necessarily start in mid-March – the preparations are already beginning . . . when, exactly? Now, during the winter, when the first bulbous, sticky, fat buds appear? Or sooner, in the autumn, when the old is expelled to facilitate preparations for the new? Surely it must be the summer, when all is basking, receptive, erect and fertile. Or I wonder if it is the spring itself – nature's foreplay – which lays down its own blueprint for self-replication a year hence. Our barriers between the seasons and their own peculiar functions are simply arbitrary, nominal conventions, and within each lies at least a strand from all of the others.

We wandered about aimlessly with the intention of putting some floral faces to names and vice versa. There was a lot of stuff that we recognized visually, from gardens in other places and times, only to realize that it was something that we had also heard of but not seen. There were, of course, plants which both of us had neither seen nor heard of before, but not a great deal. Not according to all the crap we spouted anyway. Show me a pansy right now, and I'd probably tell you it was a begonia. For all I know, they are different names for the same plant, which would make me look doubly stupid.

One flower I spied was an iris, Pauline, which, according to my journal, is 'rather lovely and kind of leopard-spotted'. The undeniable campness of which leads me neatly and mincingly on to my next train of thought. As we were strolling about, leathers on, helmets in one hand, the other being used to point out 'rather lovely, leopard-spotted' flowers to each other, I realized that Steve and I were gay. We're not gay, de facto, and I am at pains to point out that if we were, we wouldn't be ashamed or embarrassed to admit it. Come to think of it, if I *was* gay, I would probably quite fancy Steve. Over coffee ('Sugar, or are you feeling sweet enough today, gorgeous?') we gazed seductively and dreamily into each other's eyes as we discussed our burning desire not only for each other, but also for a greenhouse. I have a feeling that this urge is based more on the worry that as soon as the shed is up we will no longer have anything to build, than on the fact that we actually need one or know how to use it. It also relates to the notion I have lodged in my mind that you're not a proper gardener until you have a greenhouse. It denotes a certain seriousness – an air of dedication. You have somehow gone beyond the rather grubby and prosaic activity of simply dumping things in the soil (not that we've done that yet either), and have decided to incorporate some of the altogether more genteel and sophisticated horticultural arts, such as marrow manipulation, cucumber coercion and tomato tuning into your repertoire. It's another way of getting more involved with the life cycle, and therefore with the planet. It is somewhere else to potter, and possibly even fettle.

The *reasons* for us wanting a greenhouse are, however, entirely irrelevant, as we are both utterly broke, and therefore the likelihood of us getting one in the near future is nil. Unless we steal one, and I don't fancy our chances of doing that on the bike. Those ghastly helmets play havoc with your hair at the best of times.

On the way out, I stopped to make a note of the prices and varieties of their seed potatoes.

First Earlies: Home Guard, Organic Premiere, Concorde, Swift, Epicure, Rocket, Maris Piper, Duke of York, Foremost, Arran Pilot.
Second Earlies: Wilja, Kestrel, Catriona.

Maincrops: King Edward, Desiree, Pentland Crown,
Majestic.
All at £3.99 for a 2.5 kg bag.

Checking the records from November, when we decided
which potatoes we wanted to grow (decisions based
largely on which ones looked either nice or least likely
to be killed by us), I can see that they have our chosen
first earlies (Maris Piper or Foremost), we are stuffed
for second earlies, and okay for Mains – King Edward.
We'll need to do some hunting around to find what we
need at the right prices – these seemed a little steep to
me.

This kind of conjecture is one of the great joys of
gardening – it allows me the luxury of spending half an
hour or so weighing up the pros and cons of potato
varieties. This in turn reminds me that I must acknowledge my gratitude that I am one of the luckier of the
world's population by virtue of having enough food to
eat on a regular basis, let alone being able to choose
which varieties of potatoes to grow, as opposed to
worrying about how I will feed my family if they do not
grow at all.

I drew no real conclusions, potato-wise, and Steve
wasn't much use either, giving me his usual 'sounds
good', or 'whatever, mate', as he does when I ask him
pretty much anything. While we rode to Sainsbury's to

forage for processed food, I found myself wondering how many seed potatoes it took to make 2.5 kg, trying to figure out how big and/or dense they were in relation to my fist and then estimating how many of my fists I could get inside one of those netting bags. I would have asked at Hillier's, but I was afraid that I might get one of those withering looks which usually follows a rhetorical question such as 'How long is a piece of string?' The answer to which, of course, is 'Twice the length of the middle to the end.'

We hunted fromage frais and gathered corn flakes before heading home, where Lizzie, like the angel she is, had baked potatoes dolloped with big lumps of 'I can't believe it's another marketing scam *light*', tuna mayonnaise and grated cheese waiting for us. Over lunch, we compared mornings, with Lizzie seeming to think that four hours of researching an essay for her MA in Social History had been tougher than our morning of apologizing and being gay.

The lunch hour had seen a low and ominous-looking cloud billowing itself out like a damp grey sheet just over where we wanted to be digging, but by the time we got to the plot it had passed over to ruin someone else's day. Last night's fairly sharp frost had lost its keenness, making the soil workable, if a little sticky. Last October, when we originally dug the bed we were going to attack today (bed 'e' – possibly swedes), we had been perhaps less concerned with creating a healthy growing environment than with making it look like we had done something, in the same way that some people shuffle pieces of paper around their desk without reading or acting upon them. But, like paperwork, couch grass grows if you do nothing about it, and it seems to especially like growing in the middle of winter when deprived of light by the bloody great tarpaulin which we covered this particular bed with a couple of months ago, weighed down with a dozen or so half-bricks. Any plant which can survive that kind of treatment and is not edible has no place on our plot. It all had to come out. As we dug, we discussed whether it would be possible to develop some kind of hybrid plant, combining the utility and taste of vegetables with the vigour and tenacity of weeds. We reckoned a fortune could be made out of the seed packet bearing the following instructions:

Sow anywhere, in any kind of soil. Whenever. Particularly likes cracks in paving slabs. Sun or shade, sheltered or exposed; needs no thinning. When young, tread and fork into the soil. Leave well alone, do not feed, water or fertilize. Cover and protect from light and nutrients.

If dandelions and couch grass can manage it, then surely potatoes could be persuaded to follow suit.

Ted interrupted our digging to, in his own words, 'check we were getting on with it' and to tell us, quite by chance, that his neighbour had a greenhouse on offer – free to anyone who'd take it away – if we wanted it. He gave me his own phone number, which I jotted down on my palm-top (the back of my hand) with a biro. Steve and I tried, and probably failed, to not look like two excited schoolboys, while I told Ted that I would call him to arrange a time to come and look at it (what am I going to do? Suck my teeth, kick its frame and tell him it's not worth it, not without an MOT?). Again, and again foolishly, Steve has entrusted the inspection to me, partly as he has to work for the next few days, but mainly because I know a little bit more about greenhouses than he does – namely, that the pointy bit goes at the top.

Ted disappeared again. On the way to his car, he brought forth flame from a fire which he lit some three weeks ago and which had, to all visible intents and purposes, been dead for a fortnight, simply by singing to it. His arrival had broken our rhythm, so we used him as an excuse to stop for the day. We did the usual circuit around the park before a fresh-eyed last glance at the results of our labours. We had done a good job – it had been twenty minutes, and still there were no weeds. I extricated Charlie from the predicament he found himself in with the amorous and/or psychotic but entirely harmless attentions of the local loony German Shepherd, Rachel, and waddled home – I still had four jumpers, a leather jacket, two pairs of trousers and a full-face helmet on. I thought the digging had been making me sweat more than usual.

This evening, I wanted to work out how many seed potatoes we are going to need. *The Vegetable Garden Displayed* suggests that tubers 'the size of a large egg' weigh approximately 2–3 oz. This is particularly unhelpful in its ambiguity, as not only does it not give any indication as to what they consider 'large' in terms of eggs, but also omits to say from which bird the egg has fallen. Ordering what you thought were tubers the size of a quail's egg, only to be confronted with something which would not shame a goose, or even an ostrich, would be disastrous. Secondly, this piece of information does not stipulate whether the ounces in question are Troy or Avoirdupois. It may not seem like much, but over a few pounds mistakes can accumulate. However, and notwithstanding other people's sloppiness, I think I've managed to figure it out. We need ninety earlies and ninety maincrops to fill our needs and our potato bed, which sounded about right and more or less tallied with my calculations involving fists in netting sacks (which curiously and deviously reminds me of iris Pauline). One thing concerns me, though: that's about six bags of Hillier's finest, which is twenty-four bloody quid. This in turn must surely beg questions regarding how many spuds you could buy from Tesco's for that much, and would they last us the winter?

10 A Good Life

Tying the Ted Hitch

5 February

It is first thing in the morning. To me, today, this means about 9.30. The next twelve hours or so seem so cram-full of things to do that they look like the panes in one of those how-many-people-can-you-squeeze-into-a-phone-box record attempts, the twisted faces of my errands bent-nosed and flat-cheeked against the steaming glass. I initially sat down to work out how many onions we are going to need, but after last night's battle with the potatoes I'm not sure I have the heart for it. The mixture of a Protestant work ethic and Catholic guilt is a heady brew – luckily I have overcome both, and I work when I feel like it, for however long it takes. But I do find it very difficult to do literally nothing – I'm fine if there is information either coming in or going out, but when the stuff inside my head starts swirling around like dry leaves trapped in a wind-eddy – a cerebral vortex – I get bored and frustrated. So I started writing about anything that wasn't to do with counting onions in order that I could avoid not only that, but also thinking about all the other things I should be doing.

Onions. I was thinking that I should maybe get some onion seeds going in the propagator. This was a very kind and somewhat surprising Christmas gift from the mother of a friend – a lady who has always given the impression that she has, at best, ambivalent feelings towards me. I spoke to my college friend George in Loughborough at the weekend and my call had, she said, interrupted her sowing her seeds. She knows a good deal more about allotments, and onions, than I do, so I guess I should get some in as well. Good grief, I'm even writing about the things that I have to do as a displacement activity. It must be bad. It's about to get worse.

There is also some wildly sprouting garlic in the pantry which could do with being planted either roundly outside or squarely in the middle of a curry. The chances of me cooking anything as exotic as this or indeed anything involving more than a plastic tray and a bag of salad in the next week or so are like the story of the virgin birth – inconceivable. So outside it is for it. But where? The books say that garlic likes a good amount of sunshine – not a problem as the 'garden' is predominantly south-facing. But the 'garden' is also a mess, and isn't going to get any better without a good deal of stomping, burning and humping stuff about, during which I can foresee lots of quite promising livid-green garlic spears also being stomped and burnt, if not humped. What to do? Ah well, no doubt the day will unfold as it should. Maybe I could help it to unfurl by slipping down another cuppa, then taking Charlie out to kill some fluffy bunnies – that usually concentrates the mind.

6 February

It feels as if it's been a really busy couple of days. Probably because it has. This is good, and certainly better than daytime television. The net result of all this activity is that I am finally sitting down to write at 10.35 in the evening, which isn't the easiest time to remember what I've actually done in the last twenty-four hours, let alone recount it.

Yesterday turned out to be somewhat disjointed – a bit of compost fettling, some writing and the odd dig here and there. Of all these things, it is the compost which has given me the most satisfaction (a sentence which stands as further proof that I am indeed turning into my late father). I'm chuffed about the compost, though, because it seems to be looking and smelling as it should – of nothing. I like to think that this is because of our diligence in adding exactly 10 per cent screwed-up paper (compost is like us – it needs fibre) and the fact that we pour good honest piss on it on a regular basis (I would hate to subject it to bad, devious piss). Whatever it is, we seem to be doing something right because the bottom of the bin is full of well-broken-down stuff which doesn't smell like a pigsty. It is also riddled with worms which is another good sign. It is becoming increasingly apparent, however, that the green plastic upside-down-bin-without-a-bottom-but-a-lid-at-the-top-if-you-see-what-I-mean-compost-thingy which we inherited is not going to be of sufficient capacity to swallow the combined output of both our households. In other words, it's useless and we're going to need something much bigger for the amount of crap our kitchens produce. So I've made a new one. It's a monster. Well, it looks like one in the garage, as it takes up all the spare floor space. Granted, there isn't much of that at the moment anyway, occupied as it is by the bits of wood which are soon to be a shed. The bin is about 8 feet by 3 feet in plan, and about 2 feet high, divided into three sections. It has been lovingly hand-crafted using only the very finest bunk-bed and garage-door pine, some screws and a claw hammer. Unfortunately the uprights of the beds did not have pineapple finials or ball and claw feet, which I thought would have looked magnificent. I did, however, very deliberately make sure that the number 3 of the garage door remained visible as a proud nod to, and a reminder of, its provenance.

After I'd carefully hammered in a hundred or so screws in an attempt to give the bin a chance of standing up straight, I feasted on bent nails and sawdust before heading up to the plot with Charlie in order to remove the rest of the rocks and weeds that Steve missed a couple of days ago. I was also going so that I could indulge in my new leg-toning exercise regime of carrying half the plot's topsoil around on my boots.

Luckily, Ted arrived about half an hour after I did. He 'mustn't stop' but informed me that he had spoken to his neighbour about the greenhouse, and he would indeed be extremely grateful if someone would come and remove its oxidized frame and randomly shaped pieces of glass from his garden, and would I like to go and look at it this afternoon? Tough call – stay here and continue to squelch my way through a couple more rows of soil you could make pots out of, or go and give our gleaming new tomato palace the once-over?

Ted gave me directions: 'You know as you're driving through the village, after the school, there's a right turn?'

'I know it – Bourne Lane, isn't it?'

Ted nodded his way through this sentence while holding his cap still, and simultaneously mouthed 'Bourne Lane' in affirmation.

'Well it's not that one, but the next one.' He gestured by leaning to his left and pointing to two different imaginary locations in mid air with his onion-skinned forefinger.

'You mean Northfields?'

'That's it!'

He seemed as impressed by my local knowledge as anyone who had lived here roughly fifty times longer than me would, but I think that having to explain to me twice where to go after that right turn took the edge off this. We arranged to meet at his place an hour hence which, I thought, should give me just enough time to remember how to get there, or at least drive around for long enough to happen upon it.

Seeing Ted without his tweed flat-cap came as something of a surprise. I think I had half expected that the hair at the sides and the back of his head came off with it, like the combined Tam O' Shanter and ginger wig which parodies and patronizes the 'Scotsman'. Ted's cap and snowy hair somehow seem to distil the essence of 'Allotment Master'. But the hat is, of course, a part of his uniform and it follows that it comes off at home. Without it, Ted has a shock of thick, pure white hair. He is a handsome, kind and gentle-looking man, with eyes so blue that they should have been at sea all their life, but I think they've spent most of it on a tractor. When he answered the door, I momentarily thought that I had indeed forgotten his directions, and had come to the wrong house.

'Ted, you've got hair!' was what I probably should not have said, but did. He blinked and smiled at me in a patient but vaguely patronizing way before eagerly showing me his garden, and in particular the snap-line straight brick wall which one of his sons had built to keep the soil in one half of the garden (a raised lawn) from collapsing onto the other half (a sunken patio). I don't blame him for his pride – it's a very tidy job, as is the rest of his garden – compared to mine it's like Hampton bloody Court.

Anyway, the greenhouse looked fine. The pointy bit is at the top at both ends, the door slides from closed to half open, and with a bit of persuasion from some oil and a mallet could probably be made to open to nearly three-quarters if not more. Besides, it's free, and by moving it we're doing Chris (Ted's neighbour) a favour, so, if only on altruistic grounds, it is utterly justifiable. And I'm sure it will look fabulous next to the knackered old motorbike which I nearly thought about renovating just after I paid someone fifty quid for the pleasure of getting it out of his way a few years ago. This has been languishing in the 'garden' (not just this one – I've actually bothered to move it twice) ever since, having long ago attained 'sculpture' status.

My life has been quite literally littered with these random acts of space-kindness. The most spectacular, I think, being the alleviation, in 1997, from a then colleague, of two lovely wooden sailing boats, which for some reason he didn't want any more (probably because they were peppered with holes and had no sails). They did, however, provide my then wife and me with seemingly endless hours of happy viewing from the kitchen window, as they gracefully slipped from 'unseaworthy' to 'unmovable' in front of our eyes.

Ted and I made some arrangements regarding moving the greenhouse, involving his other son, a pick-up truck, some rope and a sense of humour. By chance, I met Kevin a couple of days ago at the park as we were both dog walking. We seemed to get on well enough in a blokey and easy sort of way, so I reckoned that he'd be up for it. We figured that taking the greenhouse apart before moving it was only asking for trouble, and reasoned that putting it straight onto the back of the pick-up would be just fine.

Before I left Ted said, apropos of something which escapes me now, that he'd had 'a good life'. He said this with the middle-distance gaze of an elderly man who could see it all laid out before him like a miniature town full of warm avenues and familiar back roads. For me to get to seventy-four at all will, I think, be remarkable enough in itself, but to get there being able to sum it all up as 'good' would do me just fine, so hats off to Ted and, for that matter, to anyone else with hair as impressive as that.

11 The Little Shop of Allotments

The Littlest shed

9 February

The end of what those who have a week call the weekend. I spent the day helping to remove a hundred years or so of wallpaper from a friend's mother's bedroom walls. I didn't feel as if I had much choice – she *did* buy me the propagator after all. I wondered, but didn't ask, as we scraped, hacked and very occasionally peeled, whether anybody else was thinking about how, as each sliver was pulled from the next, we were increasing the overall volume of the room. Imperceptibly, but undeniably. A little like pissing in the ocean making the tide higher, or Steve's digging making the plot look any better. I felt similarly loath to ask them whether they thought that there was no more in the bin bags than the rips, flakes and strips of harlequin patterns, or if we might also be discarding a hundred years or so of skin and memories which had been sucked into the pores of the paper.

So, while tomorrow looms in the minds of many as some kind of suit-encrusted endurance test, I am faced with a dilemma of my own which I am sure many would not envy – should I set the seed potatoes out to chit, or finally get some onion seed in the propagator? Doing the former will involve a good deal of manoeuvring in the garage involving sheets of plywood and egg boxes, while getting onions on the go will necessitate finding everything I need for the job, i.e. the propagator, onion seeds, trays, compost, cotton bud (for use as a dibber), and a pair of digital Vernier calipers to measure compost depth and seed spacing. Each activity has its merits and drawbacks – putting potatoes in boxes strikes me as the option for the brain dead or psychopathic, making it perfectly acceptable as far as I'm concerned, but the satisfaction – excitement even – of neatly sowing onion seeds in a 6 x 7 grid is a truly mouth-watering prospect. However, that's tomorrow. There's some catching up to do.

After I got back on Friday, having taken the boys over to their mother, I found myself wondering why I felt a sudden and strong urge to go and see Steve. Was it because I wanted to express to him how much I value his loyal and rock-like friendship? It didn't sound likely. Perhaps we had recently arranged to meet up, but I could only remember the conversation's echo, so simply had a nagging feeling that I was supposed to go and see him. I didn't know. I thought, drank tea, scratched my head and assumed all manner of catalogue-man poses, brow furrowed, chin cupped, plain-glass spectacles placed sagely on the bridge of my nose, but it was no good. There was only one thing to be done – two, counting going round on foot – but it was raining. Steve and Liz's answering machine wheezed and spluttered its way into action and I heard, surely for the thousandth time, Liz's very valiant attempt to sound as if she really cared who was calling, what they wanted and what their phone number was.

'Stevie, it's m—'

'What d'you want, you dickhead?'

'Steve, you got any beer in the fridge?'

Of course! Why else would I want to go and see him?

*

Once we were sitting comfortably, we realized that there were indeed a few other matters which we ought to discuss. I wanted to find out which shifts he was working next week so I knew when I could go round and watch their telly, have a bath and steal some food. We needed to address the greenhouse situation in terms of what we had to get for it (namely, everything except the aluminium bits) and when would be a suitable delivery day for the frame. I also wanted to show Steve the new plans of the plot I'd drawn up, as well as the compost bin, which was still in the garage looking enormous, in flat-pack form, but tied together with string to show it off. Also on the agenda was the matter of the rotten grass clippings from last year's cricket season which are languishing on the other side of the park. I have no idea whether or not they are any good for the soil, but it strikes me that all other rotten vegetation is, and I've read that it's good to put grass cuttings on compost, and anyone who writes a book about gardening must know what they're talking about, right?

So, Steve shuffled his (cigarette) papers, and called the meeting to order by retying his ponytail and lighting a roll-up. Unsurprisingly, there were no apologies. We discussed matters in no more detail than was absolutely necessary, digressed as and when we felt like it, popped round to my garage to kick the new compost bin, laughed a lot and said things like 'that's fine by me', 'whatever, mate', 'you know best' and 'sounds good'. There was no other business. The minutes, had anyone bothered to take any, would have read 'SN inspected the new compost bin and was most complimentary, with particular reference to how well the screws had been hammered in. RS said nothing of any great note about the greenhouse or anything else, with which SN wholeheartedly agreed. SN and RS agreed that they should buy some seed potatoes the next morning.'

And so it was that 10.15 yesterday morning saw us stamping our boots onto flat concrete and blowing into cupped hands in an attempt to stay conscious. It was so cold that not only could we see the clouds of our own breath, but also that they were solidifying in front of us, falling to the ground and smashing. We were surveying the daunting array of seed potatoes in the 'Winchester New Allotment Society Limited Trading Shed', an establishment at the entrance to the Park Road allotments just outside Winchester to which Sue Harris, our allotment society secretary, had directed us, abbreviating it to 'The Allotment Shop'. No wonder we couldn't find it. Had we stopped and asked three separate people if they could direct us to the 'Winchester New Allotment

Society Limited Trading Shed', rather than grunting something about an allotment shop, I'm sure we would have found it seconds, possibly even minutes, sooner.

The place in question actually seems to be doing itself something of a disservice by calling itself a 'shed', as it is considerably larger and more sturdy than this. However, 'shop', in any other than the most functional of senses (four walls, a roof and things you can buy), is itself a little too plush a word. It is somewhere between the two – a brutally utilitarian building with a concrete floor and interrogation lighting, where it is possible, from what I could glean, to buy pretty much everything any allotment-holder could dream of – from pea netting to pH testing kits, and from pots to our very reason for being there – potatoes.

We had been a little concerned about the notice nailed to the door of the shack which effectively informed us that non-members could bugger off and get their spuds from Tesco's like everyone else. So we entered with a little trepidation and some questions about becoming members, please, if that's not too much trouble. The two folk – one male, one female – behind the counter looked for all the world as if Edward Hopper had painted them after having spent a good amount of time leafing through an Hieronymous Bosch book – as if they had pensively grown where they stood and had become wise but weary, forlorn but ever hope-ful. They studied us with a synchronized, ambiguous smile that said one of three things – either that they were about to sell us something that we did not know we wanted, or that they were about to eat us or, simply, 'she's behind you'.

We grinned back inanely, as if to say 'Oh no she isn't!'

'Can I help you?'

As we jumped, we also turned, and were faced with an elderly, red and shiny lady who was all coats and smiles and bobble-hats and, going by the look in her eyes, full of the unmitigated joys of potato vending. Either that, or she also wanted to eat us. As we stared at our shuffling and uncomfortably numb feet, we mumbled about how we would like to become members and how Sue Harris had sent us and she said it would be all right if we came an—

'Sue *who*?'

Oh shit. She is going to eat us.

'Er, Sue *Harris*?'

'What does she look like?'

Her eyes had gone all Patrick Moore on us. She had us stumped here. What *did* Sue look like? Of course, we could picture her in our mind's eye but, like a word you use every day but cannot define when asked to by a child, we could not find a way of explaining it. I realized that to say that all old people look the same is about as morally, intellectually and socially acceptable as saying the same about any other sector of society but, let's face it, 'elderly, white hair, glasses, wears a grey overcoat' doesn't exactly narrow it down when it comes to your average allotment demographic description.

Patrick helped us out,

'Elderly lady, white hair, glasses, grey coat?'

'That's her!'

'Oh well, that's all right, then – you're associate members. You're one of us.'

I think that we were both dubious about this accolade, especially when the two behind the counter clapped their hands and gurgled this last phrase excitedly, mentioning something about not having eaten – sorry – *seen* an associate member since 1948. And I'm not convinced that Patrick had any more of an idea who Sue Harris was than before, but I got the impression that she had figured that, although we may have looked a bit different from most others who came into their shop, we did not seem to pose any kind of threat and that our money was as good as anyone else's, even if it was decimal. Besides, there's not much meat on either of us, so we left the Winchester New Allotment Society Limited Trading Shed with smiles, cheery farewells, all of our limbs and an awful lot of potatoes which had cost half what they would have done from most garden centres.

Apparently, the reason that we had been eyed with suspicion at first was because the members always put in their orders late in the year preceding the growing year. They therefore have only a limited supply for clueless hippies like us, so our turning up and demanding two hundredweight of Pink Fir Apples was never likely to go down too well.

Whichever way we wangled it, we now have 7 lb. each of the following: Foremost, Maris Piper and Pink Fir Apple. Foremost because their name will remind us to dig them up first, Maris Piper because everybody has heard of them, so they must be okay, and Pink Fir Apples because Christopher Lloyd reckons that they are all that is worth growing, potato-wise, and consequently remind me of my sister, Jacq, who bought me one of his books for Christmas. It's such a dainty name for such an earthy, knobbly, lumpy and frankly ungainly entity (not Jacq, the potato). No self-respecting potato has wispy words like 'pink' or fruity ones like 'apple' in its name. Potatoes should have dependable names like Doris or Brian. For some reason, I had mistakenly taken Pink Fir Apples to be earlies, only because they sound like they should be (not in the literal dig-these-up-first sense of Foremost, but in the more nebulous we-sound-a-bit-delicate-so-you'd-better-keep-us-in-that-nasty-rough-soil-for-as-little-time-as-possible way of things). But I am, I have just discovered, wrong. Late maincrops, actually, so really very wrong. At least I found out now rather than in mid-June, when we would have found ourselves digging up pink fir crab-apples instead.

So, that was the so-called weekend. Apart from removing about 10,000 cubic millimetres of wallpaper, today I have done nothing more interesting than fitting a thermometer to the inside of the propagator lid in readiness for onion sowing, and moving some wood around in the garage to facilitate access to the bench under the window at the back where the potatoes are going to sprout. I still haven't decided which I am going to do first. I think I'll leave it until I've got the morning and a clear head to choose. Right now, I've got a hundred years of paste and memories to wash off my skin.

12 Bloody Cats

All the Right-Way Up

10 February

One of the joys of commencing any new activity is the
quantity, and often quality, of subject-specific new
words to be learned. In the case of gardening, one of
the best, to my ear, is 'tilth'. It also allows me to use
such undulating sentences as 'I laid my tubers out to
chit this afternoon', which I would dearly love to hear
Stephen Fry saying. I did not do this first thing, though,

nor did I sow onions as I said I might, because when I woke up the sun had been switched on. Not to full, but about gas mark 4, or 'bottom aga' round here, I suppose. In any event, it was too pleasant for there to be any excuse not to put up the compost bin. Or, as I prefer to call it after our visit to the Winchester New Allotment Society Limited Trading Shed, the 'Patented Bedstead Three Stage Kitchen Waste Recycling Unit'.

As I drank my first cup of tea of the morning I forced down a bowl of muesli, the Shakespeare of breakfast cereals – wholesome, worthy, but frankly rather dull. I am now grateful, though, that I chewed through a good part of *King Lear* and at least three acts of *Othello*, otherwise I'd be mighty hungry. Muesli? Not very moorish? Thought not. Could do with another cuppa, though. To distract myself from this epicurean tedium, I performed a visualization of the procedures necessary to build the bin. This way, as I reached for, say, a hammer inside my mind, I could jot down a list of all the materials and equipment I would need. I've had too much experience of trying to kick nails in or use my teeth to crank screws because of a forgotten tool. This visualization technique is excellent in theory and works, apparently, for many top sportspeople. But I'm not sure the same is true of top compost-bin makers.

It was all good up to the point where I was holding

two pieces of wood together with my hands while having my right knee wedged against another plank to keep it in place. My slippery left boot was holding something else down which didn't want to stay there, I had dribbly screws dangling from my mouth, the drill-driver was just out of reach of any limb, there was a maddening itch between my shoulder blades and I desperately wanted to sneeze. Only I could make such a balls-up of a job without actually starting it. For the real thing I could tell I was going to need Steve: between us we could balls it up properly. As Steve was inconsiderately and, by his own admission only nominally, at work, I had to come up with something else to do. I figured that if I could not get the bin up today, then the least I could manage was to prepare the ground where it's going to sit. Not strictly necessary, but an awful lot more productive than watching *Bargain Hunt*. So I dragged myself and Charlie up here to the plot.

The car park is usually quiet at this time of day and this time of year, but as I walked down the path adjacent to the allotments, I noticed four cars, neatly lined like an unthemed paint chart. I figured that, as it is such a bright and relatively warm morning, a few dog walkers or ramblers were using the park as a launching point.

I am here in order to make some level ground for the new compost bin. The first task was to clear off the designated area (just below the potato patch to the east side of the plot) and to mark it out so that I can be sure of the area I am dealing with. I took some bits and pieces of debris, which I had missed previously, to the communal bin in the car park, which also gave me a view of the tennis courts. I noticed that there was a doubles match in progress, and smiled to myself as I concluded that I would far rather be digging right now.

Making a level base for the bin was to be, I reckoned, slightly easier than doing so for the shed, and would certainly involve more 'relaxed' tolerances. We don't have to be as fussy about the engineering of the compost bin as we do about the shed for the following reasons:

A. The shed is taller than the compost bin, and subsequently has a higher centre of gravity. This means that any deviation from flat at the base becomes magnified as the height increases. This is borne out by Barker's Law in mathematics, which I have just invented to add a little gravitas.

B. The shed will hold items of (marginally) higher value than the compost bin, and will therefore carry slightly higher consequences in the case of failure.

C. The shed has, so far, been free. Therefore it needs all the help it can get.

It's been simple this morning really – I heaved out a few more of our hopelessly inverted swards (another cracking word) from the adjacent bed and chucked them inside the just-a-little-larger-than-the-bin rectangle of blue nylon string I stretched between four rusty old pieces of angle bracket, and 'bingo!' – somewhere flat(ish) for the compost bin to sit. A doddle.

And yes, the four cars did belong to the quartet of tennis players, and no, none of them had given any of the others a lift, nor thought of walking or cycling here. By the time I, mighty Eco Warrior Man (who still shops at Tesco's) had WALKED home (the very thought that I would ever drive up to the plot), I had already decided that it was to be potatoes, not onions. I can't really remember why. I think it was something to do with feeling that we might be a bit late in setting out the spuds already, whereas the packet says 'March' for the onions. Also influencing my decision was the fact that all I have right now to sow seeds in is some decidedly grumpy-looking home-made compost left here by a previous resident, which I really didn't think would be up to the demands of seed nurturing.

What I thought it might be up to, however, is growing garlic – the stuff that was still sprouting incontinently in the pantry and still had not made it into a curry. I thought that it may as well take its chances in the 'garden', and that the potatoes could wait for another hour or so.

I bloody hate cats. Well, I don't actually hate cats (although I do think that they are generally aloof, indifferent, manipulative, opportunistic and devious little sods) but I do detest what comes out of their rear end and, even more specifically, what they proceed to do with it. I am as incensed as anyone else when dog owners do not clear up after their hounds – especially when it is in the middle of the park, you are playing footie with the kids and a foul becomes, well, really foul. But at least dogs have the honesty and decency to leave the stuff where it is. It would be more helpful, true, if their crap was fluorescent pink and had a sandcastle flag in it with 'danger – shit' written on it, but at least they don't try to hide it by burying it like cats do. And where have all the neighbourhood cats decided to do just that? That's right, in my bloody compost heap, that's where. Little Bastards. Devious little bastards at that.

I eventually got round to putting the garlic in. I say 'eventually' as obviously I had to sift all the cat shit out of the compost first, along with a few dozen clumsy but surprisingly sharp triangles of terracotta pot which someone had thoughtfully added just to make the job even more pleasant. As I opened out each clove-sized hole in the compost with my left index finger, wiggling it slightly on the way in to loosen the soil under where the roots were going to be, I somehow felt that what I was doing was faintly ridiculous – that I was being silly and that garlic came from shops, not out of the ground. It seemed that I was doing something which went so very diametrically against the 'you don't get anything for nothing' school of thought that it had to be wrong. 'So,' I thought, 'I take one of these gibbous, pungent, parchment-wrapped lumps, bung it in some soil, make sure it doesn't dry out and in a few months' time I can come and dig up 8–10 times what I put in.' Pure magic. It also struck me that, for the first time since I was a child of ten or so with my father in the garden, I was taking responsibility for the continuation, as opposed to the termination, of the life cycle of a vegetable. I don't want to get all stupid about this by suggesting that decapitating a carrot is bad karma, but being more holistically involved with this life cycle must surely lead to a greater understanding of it, and of the fact that not all burials are endings. Anyway, garlic's in.

Finally, I got to the potatoes. On the way home from the plot I had popped in to see Paul, the friendly landlord of the Phoenix Inn (where Glenda plays the piano on Tuesday nights), and he very kindly donated four egg trays to the cause. Together with the other egg boxes I've collected, that gave us a total PCC (potato chitting capacity) of 165, which I reckoned should easily accommodate what we bought on Saturday. I thought of counting them all, but realized that this was the sort of activity usually only carried out by obsessive little geeks. Seven pounds of Foremost equates to 38 tubers; the same weight of Pink Fir Apple and Maris Piper comes out at 52 and 44 respectively – 134 spuds aren't going to fill the plot, but with another bag of earlies and a couple more egg boxes we should be laughing.

The process of laying them out was highly entertaining, falling as it did into one of my 'all-time fun things to do' categories. This particular one being 'putting things into other things the right way up, so that none of them fall over, and so they all fit'. Everyone should try it (I don't get out much. Glenda and her piano on the occasional Tuesday is about the length of it for me). It is a similarly satisfying process to washing up. All those serried, ordered ranks of clean and bubbly things where there was once a pile of dirty, disorganized chaos. Lovely.

As I laid the potatoes out, I had a similar epiphany to that with the garlic earlier. I was trying to make sure that I had each one the right way up before putting it into its compartment – eyes uppermost, reaching blindly skyward. And then I realized – these potatoes have a *right way up*. Therefore, *all* potatoes have a right way up. Previous to this my only criterion for potatoes was that they were cooked, preferably using a lot of olive oil, garlic, sea salt and rosemary. Failing that, in a bag, deep-fried and chip-shaped with salt and vinegar. Somehow the fact that potatoes have a right way up makes them less humble – it confers some kind of elevated status upon them. It accords them more respect. I like to think so anyway.

I'm off to the Phoenix. Unfortunately Glenda (a whole lexicon of tunes, from Abba to the Beatles, plus requests) isn't there until tomorrow, but at least conversation is easier. I was in there last week and started to tell the chap sitting next to me at the bar about how many of my fists I could fit into a netting potato bag. I don't think he could quite hear me, as he just gazed into the middle distance and supped his pint. I think he may have been sympathizing with Glenda as she was reaching her crescendo of a particularly moving rendition of 'Yesterday'.

13 Kitchen Scraps and Soul Food

The impossibility of stench in
the mind of somebody clean

13 February

The compost bin is finished. At last. How long it will
stand up is anyone's guess, but it seems sturdy enough
to hold a few apple cores and bags of carrot peelings,
and that's good enough for me. It struck me, while we
were banging and cursing, that for once I was not
involved in making some kind of Art – as I have been,
on and off, for the last fifteen years or so. I am still

doing what may be termed 'creative' things – growing stuff (hopefully), writing, taking photos, researching, etc., but it is no longer Art, and for that I am truly glad. There are only so many 'statements' you can make without feeling as if you are starting to repeat yourself, and that nobody actually cares. The act of clobbering together what used to be two bunk beds and some old garage doors is as far from gesturing or posturing or even proselytizing as I think I can get, and it is liberating. True, given the right context, the correct degree of spin and the appropriate arbiter of the Emperor's New Clothes, I could call it sculpture, cut through with metaphors about beds and rotting phallic vegetables (not to mention urine), but that is not what it is – it is a compost bin, and I do not have to discuss what it 'means' with anybody, nor do I have to justify its existence, or try to sell it (a good job, as it's a bit wonky). All I have to do is put kitchen scraps in it, pour pee on them once in a while and throw them on the plot next year. I feel free, and the compost bin is probably the purest piece of art I've ever made.

A little later. Recovering from the appalling stench of the contents of the green plastic compost bin which I have just transferred to the new one. It smelled somewhat as if a wild animal had eaten some horse-shit, crapped itself and then died. Last July. And then had been put on the back shelf of a car with an old wetsuit, a block of blue cheese and a pair of tramp's socks, in full sun. It was that bad – a real hand-over-mouth job, which made operating the fork interesting. Anyway, job's done now. I'm going to tidy up, throw up and then measure up the plots.

Later still. While I was measuring, I met two fellow allotment holders whose paths I'd not crossed before. First Joyce, who I think was trying to sneak past me like I usually do when I can't be bothered to talk. But I was in the mood for a chat, so I ambled to the other side of the plot, new tape measure (from the tip, 20 metres long, a bit grubby, two quid) in hand, to introduce myself. Joyce proceeded to compliment me on the state of the plot. I was at pains to point out that it had been all my own work and that I had received no help from, and indeed had never even heard of, anyone called Steve Newcombe whatsoever. We continued with the usual pleasantries about how it was a shame that the previous incumbent could not dig any more and how, yes, she did like her flowers didn't she and, no, we didn't like her flowers because we were still digging the little buggers out even now and how, yes, it *is* that time of year again. The rest of the conversation was a little lost on me, because all I could think about was how it was 'that time of year again'. For the benefit of non-gardeners (Steve and me, for example), if there is ever a pause in a conversation with a gardener, all you need say is, 'Well, it's that time of year again.' It's always 'that time of year' in any garden, and this expression will rub any gardener into a conversational lather about either digging, manuring, seed nurturing and sowing, weeding, watering, harvesting or digging (again), and any conversational awkwardness will be banished. Don't attempt this if you have any pressing appointments scheduled for the rest of the day, however. They can go on a bit.

I also met Joyce's husband, Ron – a ruddy, jolly-looking and thoroughly decent bloke from what I could gather. Their patch, he proudly informed me, was the one with the 'sentry box' shed, three plots to the north of ours. Naturally I complimented him on his handi-work, and we engaged ourselves in some beautifully blokey banter about construction techniques, doors, locks, hinges, etc. Arms folded, heads shaking and lips chuckling over phrases such as 'Oh, yeah – don't I know it' and 'How much? You must be joking!'

After they had left, I carried on measuring what turns

out to be a patch of land surprisingly regular in its rectangularity. A few moments later, Joyce returned, clutching a beige plastic carrier bag, twisted and scrunched down tight at the top. I guessed that, having admired my handiwork on the compost bin, she was donating some scraps to the cause.

'Do you like sprouts?'

Now, if I were to choose to eat a bowl of anything, then sprouts probably would not make the shortlist. Actually, that is at best a euphemism and at worst a downright lie. I loathe sprouts with a passion. When I was a child, my mother would tie me to the chair, hold my nose and stuff them into my mouth forcibly (she will, of course, deny that this ever happened). My head would spin round and round and I would spray the walls with sprouty vomit while reciting the Lord's Prayer backwards.

'Mmmmm . . . can't get enough of them, Joyce!'

In a society where many seem to want to take what they can for themselves (indeed a society which some-times appears to encourage and reward this behaviour) and don't seem so keen on giving anything back, I happen to think that it is worth taking a moment to appreciate the spirit in which some give to others. Not in expectation of reciprocation; nor out of a misplaced sense of duty, but simply because they can, and because they want to. I don't think it's going to make me like sprouts any better, but the gesture makes me like the human race just a little more, proving beyond doubt that it is the giving, rather than the given, which matters.

And on that dreary cliché, I'm off to scour the fridge for a tin of beer so I can drink to Ron and Joyce, the indomitable generosity of the human spirit and to the miracle that is the freezer, which is where the sprouts are while I think of what the hell I'm going to do with them.

14 Men Come, Make Shelter

Stevie Screws in Another Nail

19 February

We had a wild time at the Phoenix a few nights ago, blowing what remained of the shed budget on lager, followed by some 'afters' at Steve and Liz's. Without wishing to falsely portray him as someone who has any kind of problem with alcohol, it is fair to say that Steve likes his beer. It would be even fairer to assert that he likes mine a whole lot better. But surely everyone's

favourite booze is that which has been bought by someone else. It is impossible to begrudge him this, though,
particularly because I am quite sure that I have availed
myself of his Stella supply as often as he has mine.
Another reason why I like to ply Steve with beer is that
he – not the most guarded of men even when sober –
becomes as soft and vulnerable as a hermit-crab between
shells after a couple of pints and, not being binge
drinkers, thankfully the only thing that gets truly plas-
tered when we get together is the grin across Steve's
face. We like to down a few tins and, as most people
do, allow ourselves to drift further into topics of conversation than perhaps we might when our tongues are
tied a little tighter. Inevitably, we will often enter the
realms of utter hyperbole and fantasy, but Stevie is one
of the few friends I have in whose company I feel safe
to spout as much crap as I like without feeling any hint
of self-consciousness or embarrassment. Even when I
start going on about really absurd ideas, such as taking
on an allotment or building a shed, Steve has the knack
of making me believe that it is a fabulous idea, that he
is right behind me and why don't I give someone a call
about it in the morning? The answer to which, of
course, is generally, 'Because in the morning I will have
forgotten this conversation along with all the others we
have had.'

Tonight, though, I am sober – but I do have the beginnings of a fuzzy cold, so this might well make about as much sense as we did then. Monday, however, was a big day. Even Steve did some work. We sawed and hammered and swore while performing the entire gamut of erection-, screwing- and tool-based puns, so I was fully tired as well as half sozzled.

Getting the shed up, as we very nearly have, not only makes us very obviously more manly and rugged, but also means I have now cleared all that crappy, rotting wood out of the garage. This is very important, as I have a lot of other pieces of old junk in there that need to be ignored until they get in the way instead. But I'm not convinced that the car appreciated the weight of all the wood in the back and on the roof any more than it appreciates muddy wellies on its carpets – it had only just recovered from heaving the compost bin about. Since then it hasn't creaked any louder, from anywhere other than it usually does, so I guess we got away with it. We were also a little concerned that having the car so heavily laden would attract attention to ourselves, meaning that we might have had to go about our erection with half of Twyford watching, and we weren't sure if we would be up to performing with an audience. We had not done ourselves any favours in this regard last week by telling everybody who would listen where and when we would be attempting this feat. The responses were varied, but reading between the furrowed lines they all said the same thing; 'This I have *got* to see.' Luckily they had all forgotten, though, and when we arrived the park was deserted apart from Ted, who I am slightly concerned may have taken root.

As we pulled into the car park, he did indeed raise a bemused, amused eyebrow at our improbable and ineffective lashing techniques 'securing' the load to the top of the car. These comprised a blanket, a length of old rope, four wound-down windows and Steve holding on valiantly round the corners, his knuckles white with tension and cold. The wood on the roof, had Steve's grip not been so ape-like, would have been sliding about like oiled pasta in a pan, but I reckon, considering the logistical problems we'd faced, that to have got it all up there in two car-loads by eleven o'clock without injury, falling out or even bickering was quite an achievement.

Eleven o'clock, of course, is tea time (we might have had coffee but, by now, it's difficult to tell from my flask). As we swilled, we kicked planks of wood in a knowing, domineering kind of way, and muttered to each other about four-be-twos, cross-braces and different types of nail. After, from habit, throwing away the last mouthful of cea, toffee, or whatever it was, we set to laying the base – which involved, to be fair to us, a procedure a little more complicated than simply chucking it on the ground. Only a little more complicated, but more. The base itself is fashioned from four-be-two-be-forty-eight, five of (5 pieces of 4 inch by 2 inch softwood, planed or un-planed – doesn't matter, 4 feet long) to which is screwed 24 square feet of old bunk bed. To get the base level (see Barker's Law, p.134) we had begun by stoutly and squarely placing fifteen (three for each four-be-two) house bricks on the prepared ground and checking those were level. Of course, they were as level as a llama's back to start with, but we eventually managed to pack, bed and otherwise cajole them into positions which would allow the shed to stand without wobbling like a half-set jelly. At one point, I think that we might even have given the impression that we knew what we were doing, had anyone been watching. Unfortunately, the only person watching was Ted, and he knows exactly how incompetent we are.

However, our audience was about to double. Just as we had placed the right-hand side of the frame on the base with a view to screwing it down, we heard the ominous 'squeak-DING!' of the gate being opened at the other side of the allotments. We did synchronized wincing. Only one person opens the gate as pedantically as that. Ken is also the only person to use capital letters for the 'ding'. We were actually grateful it was him, because if he hadn't arrived then who would have been there to tell us how to put up our shed? As he approached, he waved his walking stick at us and then at the beginnings of our shed.

''Ave you got plannin' permission for that thing?'

We knew, of course, that he was attempting to be humorous, as much as we knew that this would be the first thing he would say to us, and we told him as much. We then proceeded to tell him that no, we didn't have planning permission because we didn't need it, and what the bloody hell did it have to do with him anyway? We could have said just the last part of that, in truth, because, as usual, he either wasn't listening or couldn't hear us. I busied myself with drilling holes in the bottom of the shed frame while Steve held it upright at the same time as being accosted by the stick which, from what I could gather, was holding forth on computers.

I started to really listen only when it began waggling in my direction and yelled, 'If thaat wuz me doin' thaat, I'd use a waasher under thaat screw mumble dither arse piffle and then I'd mutter thing whatsit and it's called countersinkin'.'

'Well, Ken, it's not you doing it, is it? It's me, and in point of fact I am counter*boring* these holes, not countersinking them. I am doing this because the screws I have are not long enough to go through the 130 mm of wood necessary to hold it in place, and this will work perfectly well, thank you. Now bugger off and dig your plot, you interfering old windbag' made a lovely tune in my head, 'plinkety plonk, plinkety plonk', which I whistled along to as I smiled and pretended not to hear what he said. If he can get away with it then so can I.

The rest of the day passed without much in the way of major intrigue or incident, but considering the fact that we were putting up a shed on an allotment in a village which still has Bakelite telephones with four-digit numbers and a local bobby with a cape and a bicycle who clips young rapscallions round the ear for being cheeky, it was unlikely that a great deal out of the ordinary was going to happen. We got all of the framework up and covered most of the back and all of the roof with some sheets of old ply salvaged from another derelict plot. Finally, after we had screwed some battens in place on the front of the shed as supports for the window and door, we also managed to clad most of the front with the tongue and groove from the garage doors.

At this point, we became aware of three things. First, that the only way we could say with any certainty that our fingers were still attached to our hands was by looking at them, as they were far too numb with cold to even register when we were hitting them with a hammer. Secondly, there was a murmur of darkness echoing around the park. And thirdly, the pub was open. It was about six o'clock. On the way there, Steve and I talked about how, when he had finally deigned to return from cavorting around America a few weeks ago, we had taken the dogs for a walk and commented on how our quota of daylight was becoming more generous even then, light as it was until five in the afternoon. For the first time I had noticed that the transition from winter to spring, and its concomitant extra daylight, was not simply something which happened when the clocks go forward, but is expanding or contracting, little by little, every day. Tuning in to the seasons makes me realize that their wave, their rise and fall, is – along with so many other natural rhythms – a sine curve. Not a boxy square or a jagged sawtooth. Sine. Smooth. Flowing. Nature is analogue, not digital.

Yesterday morning we went back to finish off all that we could with the materials we had left – we are still waiting for the demolition crew to come and tear down the old cricket pavilion on the other side of the park to provide us with some sides which might be waterproof. The panelling I salvaged from the fence in the 'garden' will, I now realize, be about as much use for this job as papier-mâché is for making surfboards.

As well as having limited materials, we were also on a time-budget, as we had arranged to go and pick up the glass for the greenhouse after lunch. Out of the corner of my eye, I'm sure I saw the car edging further away every time we mentioned it. After collecting the glass, I had an appointment at the boys' school, after which I reckoned it would be getting dark and the pub would be open again. Not that we would be going there because, despite the fact that there was no glass in the window, the door was unhinged and still propped against the shed's half-clad framework and the roofing felt was still in my garage (the car simply closed its own boot and sped off as soon as I got near it), we managed to convince ourselves that the shed was 'finished' enough for us to drink what was left of the budget on Monday night. Consequently, because we no longer have shed money, we no longer have beer money.

Yesterday, though, we finished off the cladding on the front and also managed to hang the door the correct way up so that it opens *and* closes. While we were there, Dick gave me some clumpy, gnarly-looking raspberry roots which he had just dug up in an attempt to keep them under some sort of control. He obviously had me down as someone who had something of a dearth of uncontrollable vegetation in his 'garden', and had decided to help out. Luckily, I like raspberries a little more than I like sprouts. Just a little more, but more. Even more fortunately, I like Dick a whole lot more than I like both put together. He is a decent guy, with a fine sense of humour, by which I mean that he laughs at my jokes, so naturally I accepted his kind donation with gratitude and reciprocal good humour.

A little later, when we had run out of anything more interesting or intelligent to say, Steve brought up this subject of the kindness and altruism that we have frequently encountered since starting work on the plot. We ran through the donations we have received – bits and pieces for the shed, a petrol strimmer, sprouts, a greenhouse, raspberries, free advice and friendship. We wondered whether all of this had been down to pure luck and, if so, whether we had been responsible for making any of it ourselves by being in the right place at the right time and saying the right things to the right people. We thought that this sounded a little mercenary – as if we have manipulated situations and people to our own advantage and said only what we think others want to hear. On reflection, there may even be an element of truth to this – in office-speak I believe it's called 'people skills'. Perhaps if it is possible to concoct our own luck, then surely one of the most basic of ingredients is an ability to interact with a broad cross-section of people, respect them, their rights and their opinions and be as pleasant as possible towards them at all times. This is the enlightened path to a shed with no sides, a promise of a seized-up greenhouse with the pointy bits near the top, a bag of sprouts in the freezer incongruously wrapped in a Thornton's bag and a rapidly developing cold. Think on.

15 More Bloody Cats

Aluminium Equilibrium

The tomatoes, which I am going to grow in my bedroom in an attempt to make it smell pleasant, were chosen in memory of my father, who loved and knew his cricket, grew a fine tomato (apparently) and used to take us on holiday every year to a small, idyllic fishing village in south-west Scotland. Idyllic, that is, until I reached the age of fourteen or so, when it became a gaping chasm smack in the middle of nowhere with nothing in the way of entertainment unless you count . . . count what?

No, there really is absolutely nothing to do there. Which is probably why it is so appealing now and, no doubt, why it drew my father.

Our annual trip was never complete unless we drove up the west coast to Ayrshire, and to Culzean (pronounced 'cullayne') Castle, which I am quite sure is a fascinating jaunt for those in the market for a bit of heritage, but it bored me rigid as a pole every time. I tolerated it, though, because I was a sweet little boy who would do absolutely anything to make his dad happy, and because we got to drive past a lump of rock whose sole distinction, as far as I could gather from my father at such a tender and confused age, was that it was the same shape from whichever angle you looked at it. Even then, I had the presence of mind not to comment that yes, indeed, Father, it is just as dull from here as it was from ten miles back, and will no doubt be equally yawnsome in ten miles' time. Having said this, after spending a week or so in a small, idyllic fishing village, a lump of rock which looks the same from all angles is pretty bloody interesting, so I ogled while I had the chance – there were still to come the delights of looking round the castle and its apparently magnificent gardens, and of watching Dad spend hours with his legs akimbo while he searched for agate on a nearby beach.

That rock was called Ailsa Craig, and I'm growing

the tomatoes in memory of a man who died too soon, and who had that elusive fatherly quality of being able to elicit a 'wow' from a 'so what'. Even when we went to look at castles and lumps of rock.

No surprise, then, that six o'clock this evening saw me making holes 12.7 mm ('half an inch' just seems so lackadaisical) deep in warm, moist compost with a cotton bud and dropping a seed into each, in a 5 x 7 formation (the planned 6 x 7 didn't fit). I did two trays of onions (one of Bedfordshire Champion and one of Brunswick) and a tray of tomatoes. The latter are recognizable as being the bits that get stuck between your teeth should you have the misfortune to actually eat one of the fruits, and are a regular seed shape. If a child drew a seed, it would be one from a tomato. The onion seeds, on the other hand, are entirely different – all black and irregular, like lumps of doll's-house coal. As I dropped a seed into every one of the 35 holes in each tray, and lightly pressed the compost over them, I whispered 'night night' to each one, and read them all a story ('Jack and the Beanstalk' – something for them to aspire to), tiptoed out of the room and switched the light off. It is now 10.50 p.m., and it would be highly embarrassing to admit to the number of times I have checked on them. Fourteen.

As I popped them into their loamy caverns using a

pair of surgical tweezers (no, I'm not joking), I couldn't help smiling at the irony of what I had been doing previously. During one of those mid-cold, post-lunch, 'I actually feel like I might live' moments, I thought I might be able to turn off the World Cup cricket commentary temporarily and muster enough energy to clear a path for the imminent arrival of the greenhouse. To the rear of the 'garden' is a narrow access road, down which Kevin is going to drive his pick-up with a greenhouse frame strapped to the back of it. From there, we shall lift it over the fence using a finely balanced combination of teamwork, strategy, cunning, brute force and ignorance. Under normal circumstances this would be a breeze, as all that would stand between the pick-up and the rectangular slab of concrete on which the greenhouse is to be sited would be a low wire-mesh fence. However, there is nothing 'normal' about my 'garden', least of all its circumstances. It doesn't matter how many people you have helping you pass something that size, no matter how light it is, over any fence, no matter how low it is – if you've also got three years' worth of blackberries and bindweed in the way. So I thought that I would nip out and trim back a bit of the scrub and, well, one thing led to another and, I don't know, it all got a bit unpleasant and personal what with all the cuts and scratches – plus the fact that I was feeling a bit ropey anyway, which was obviously all the plants' fault as well. By the time I had finished it looked a little like a child's hair after it has been cut by a well-intentioned but inept parent – shorter, certainly, but not really looking any the better for it. Their clippings lay about the 'garden' looking much like what they were – detached limbs in a recent theatre of war. Back in the comfort of the utility room, crooning over the seed trays, I felt something like Dr Lecter, wiping blood from my lips with a silk handkerchief while absent-mindedly 'conducting' the cricket commentary with a cotton bud in my left hand. The blood I tasted was from my own wounds, but it felt a little odd that I had scythed and hacked at one species in order to make way for the ones whose life cycle I was just about to continue. I marvel that I am equally capable of wielding a pair of 3-foot loppers – clumsy and blunt in outcome if not in action – as I am of operating a pair of 3-inch tweezers with the dexterity and precision of an ex-jeweller. By slotting myself between these rhythms of delicate inception and violent curtailment, it feels as if I am becoming a part of that beat, and that I can start drumming. And stop fighting.

20 February

Got Dick's raspberry canes in today. Rubus idaeus, Autumn Bliss, I believe. I also believe 'Autumn Bliss' to be of similar oxymoronic value to 'Military Intelligence' or 'Sunny Scotland'. Before I could plant them, there was the small matter of finding and clearing some soil in a suitable spot (fairly sheltered, partial shade, decent, well-drained soil, near the pool). I selected a 'border' (thin rectangle of scrub) running north–south between the 'path' (coincidentally horizontal paving slabs) which leads to the rest of the 'garden' (large rectangle of scrub and more unruly slabs) and the boundary fence with the 'neighbours' (a couple who have not once, in over a year, acknowledged my existence). This choice was influenced by two factors – first, the fence is east facing, which will provide partial shade. Secondly, it is the only patch of soil in the 'garden' which isn't buried under a load of crap awaiting chemical and/or pyrotechnical warfare.

Six months ago in time, and 300 miles or so north-west in space saw me on holiday in Anglesey with my family – mother, sister, brother-in-law and my two boys. The weather, as Alan Bennett might have it, had not been kind to us, so we had to be imaginative in our choice of entertainment – a week may well be a long time in politics, but it's not nearly as long as a wet one in Wales. Going to the beach was out of the question, primarily because we couldn't actually see it.

I think it was on the Wednesday that we visited the Sea Zoo. Exactly where this establishment is escapes me, but I don't think it involved many vowels. The Sea Zoo is a fascinating place full of crabs, fish, generic plastic toys and unfeasibly large muffins. What held me most transfixed, however, was a curious outdoor sideshow, which consisted of a wooden gazebo, a bedraggled but remarkably ebullient and enthusiastic member of staff, and a few tanks housing a variety of creatures – predominantly starfish. Learning about these animals and, more to the point, what they are capable of, was something of a revelation for me – I knew that nature could be utterly extraordinary, but starfish are positively otherworldly.

Apparently, there is nothing a starfish likes to do more than to embrace a mussel shell and, prising it open with its legs, to eject its stomach into the inside of the shell in order to eat the flesh. It gets better. A starfish, if placed on its back, will use one of its five odd legs as a kind of pivot by righting it first, then cajoling the body and four remaining limbs to follow suit. The truly remarkable thing about this is that it will *always* use the same leg first. How or why anyone found this out is open to possibly grizzly speculation, but it probably came from a similar unpleasant urge to that which prompts small boys to wonder what is the minimum number of legs required by a crane fly to walk, and was almost certainly followed by an experiment to find out what happened to a starfish when it was turned upside down and had its 'pivot' leg cut off.

Speaking of which, it is relatively common knowledge that if a starfish loses one of its legs, then it can grow a new one, but what I did not realize before last August was the fact that the severed limb can, under certain circumstances, *grow a new starfish*. The lady who was running the starfish (freak)show joked that if you put a starfish in a blender, then all the little bits would grow into other starfish. She emphasized that this must not be tried at home, but she had made her point forcefully enough – that these mute and essentially blind creatures, presumably incapable of rational thought, are one of the most eloquent expressions there is of the Darwinian theory of natural selection. The same could be said of sharks or squid. Interesting how the really smart ones stayed in the water.

It may well be that the starfish, with its extreme adaptability and resilience is next in line to inherit the earth, 'waits in the jewelled basin of a pool' as John

Betjeman put it. Unless, of course, bindweed throttles it first. Bindweed, or Morning Glory as some people insist on calling at least one variety of this aberration, is the horticultural equivalent of starfish. I started on this bed for the raspberries (barely 8 feet by 18 inches) at eleven o'clock this morning, and didn't start to put the raspberries in until three this afternoon. Lunch lasted fifteen minutes. So I spent the best part of three and three-quarter hours today (not counting toilet, tea, and groaning breaks) pulling out bindweed roots. Eventually I became a little scared of the stuff – I'm sure it grew while I swigged tea, urinated and whined. The roots have the appearance of a tangled mess of cooked spaghetti, but are as brittle as the raw version, and each one-inch snap can, similarly to the dismembered leg of a starfish, grow into a whole new plant. I got out all I could find down to a depth of about one and a half forks, then decided that life was too short to go any further, and that I would wait for the rest to come to the surface, when I will be poised, shotgun in hand, and blast them into a million tiny pieces. And a million new bindweed plants.

I also discovered today that another 'weed' – yarrow – is a good companion plant for raspberries, as it deters the raspberry beetle. Also good for this purpose is garlic which, according to one of my books, 'protects the canes from a wide variety of grubs'. Can't find anything which tells me how to eradicate bindweed without either killing everything else in a 5 mile radius or digging the whole garden down to a depth of 10 feet, though – I've read that giant marigolds can cure infestations of virtually any weed, but I don't fancy its chances here after what I've seen today.

22 February

Bastard cats. Bastard bloody cats. For once, and certainly for the first time since I've been living here, it looked as if someone cared for at least a small part of the 'garden'. It even looked as if someone might have known what they were doing there, by virtue of six raspberry canes, regimentally spaced 16 to 18 inches apart, looking all military and purposeful against the only section of panelled fence which would hold their new shoots – readying themselves now to fling themselves skywards. I even went to the trouble of forking carefully around the roots of the Japanese quince nearby and dressing the whole bed with a bucket-load of the previously cat-shit-laden compost at the back of the 'garden'. It looked great. Or at least like a good start.

Then this morning, when I tiptoed out to the 'garden'

to see if there were any raspberries yet, I was confronted with dirty great holes where before there had been beautifully level, evenly firmed soil. On closer inspection, it didn't even look like the gratuitous little sods had even crapped in it. Strangely, I would have minded less if they had. But I could not help thinking that these cats knew very well what they were doing and had selected this particular piece of earth as revenge for what I wrote about them last week.

I refuse to let them get me down, though, because as of today Steve and I are the proud owners of, for want of a better description, a greenhouse. A better description might be something like 'oxidized aluminium spaceframe with the pointy bits at the top, complete with a bizarre selection of glass which looks like it was cut to fit something else'. Still, it was free, and the entertainment value of getting it here makes it worth having in a way all by itself. We met at Ted's place at 11 o'clock as arranged. The plan was to lash the frame to the back of Kevin's pick-up, whereupon he would drive the mile and a half or so to the rear access road to my 'garden' which, I discovered today, is lined with more twitching net curtains than a street full of swingers. It was as if they'd never seen a greenhouse frame on the back of a pick-up before. Kevin had brought along a friend who I initially thought was there to assist, but gradually came to realize that his chief role was that of chuckling onlooker. He accompanied Kevin in the truck, while I gave Ted a lift back to my place using the usual, but no less bumpy, access to the front. It was odd having Ted in the car – its confines seemed to startle and quiet him, like a caged bird.

Kevin arrived, and as we hoisted the frame over the fence I was glad of my efforts with the loppers the other day and made mental notes of all the things we could have tripped over had I not butchered them. I felt like pointing them out, but there are some tasks that will only ever be appreciated by yourself. The whole process went remarkably smoothly, with not a hint of the slashing, gashing, impaling, fracturing and dropping that I had envisaged. I was delighted – it had been a long time since I had added to my collection of useless and unattractive metal objects in the 'garden', so I felt that this restored some kind of aluminium equilibrium.

To help us gain purchase on the frame as it was being passed over, and because of the height discrepancy from one side to the other, I had erected one of my collapsible workbenches on the 'garden' side of the fence. When we had finished, I thanked everybody profusely and, since Kevin would not even take any petrol money from us, found out what his and Ted's preferred tipple was. I offered Ted a lift back home, but he declined as he assured me that he would be just fine squeezed into the pick-up. He then had a choice – either he could walk a quarter of a mile or so to the car, or he could climb over the fence. Being seventy-four years old did not, apparently, enter into the equation. As Ted's left foot hit the workbench, his right hand reached for the nearest fence-post; I offered my own arm as support, but his defiant look said something like 'I've jumped enough fences in my time to be able to do this one without the help of your limp wrist.' Needless to say, really, that he cleared it with ease.

So, we now have the makings of a greenhouse. It still needs some bits and bobs to finish it – glass, sealant strip, clips, time, a bloody miracle, etc., but so far it has cost us the promise of a bottle of Liebfraumilch and a four-pack of Boddingtons Bitter, which I reckon is a bit of a bargain.

16 The Warm Light of Day

The shed-to-be

23 February

It has been all of four days since I sowed those onion and tomato seeds, and have they bothered to stick any leaves out? Have they buggery. You give them all you can, and what do you get in return? It's probably my fault for inadvertently making the holes over-deep by a third of a millimetre. Or perhaps the compost granules are not of sufficiently uniform size or of high enough quality. Maybe I should sleep down there so I can keep an eye, or at least an ear, on them overnight. They're only little, after all.

To be truthful, I want to rip the top 12.7 mm of compost off and yell, 'Come on, you ungrateful little sods, get on with it – I give you water, warmth, comfort, light – what more do you want, blood, fish and bone?' I guess I just want to see if there is a real miracle happening yet – watching a tomato seed wake up and commence its remarkable but undeniable journey towards the Bolognese sauce is surely far more compelling than an apocryphal story about feeding 5,000 people with a fish and a few loaves.

The last few days have been my version of hectic, so the shed still looks much the same as it did on the night we celebrated its completion, i.e. unfinished. However, I did have a stroke of luck in that regard on Friday. I was watching Charlie chase imaginary rabbits around the park (it could have been squirrels – it's difficult to tell) when I saw two men, both of whom could be most aptly and succinctly stereotyped as 'burly', heading towards the old pavilion. On their sweaters and on their pick-up truck was emblazoned a logo which read 'Blunt Construction'. I detected from the looks in their eyes, and from the purpose with which they strode, that 'Really Quite Rude Knocking Things Down' would have been more appropriate. This was my chance. I minced my way onto a course which would intercept their manly gait and, as our paths crossed, I raised my head in one of those reverse nods which, hands in any available pockets, usually accompanies a sharp intake of breath and a greeting along the lines of 'All right?'

'All right?' They chorused as they approached.

'All right?' I replied rhetorically. In the deepest voice I could muster, I continued, 'Are you guys going to be tearing that pavilion down?' I tried not to suck my teeth as I gestured behind me.

They confirmed that they were, indeed, just on the way over to kick it's metaphorical tyres in order to ascertain exactly how obnoxious they were going to have to be towards it in order to get the job done. Judging by the size of them, I was somewhat surprised that they weren't on their way across the park to push it over by hand and then intimidate it into spontaneous architectural combustion. But they told me that they planned to commence Project Destructo the week after next and yes, I could help myself to as much wood and glass as I could eat because all they were going to do was bring it down and burn it as it stood, or rather where it used to stand.

This was a cracking result. We'll finally get some decent wood for the sides of the shed, while a little less of the old pavilion is reduced to ashes. It seemed a little sad to me. I was in the reference library only a couple of weeks ago looking at a crisp black and white photograph of three evidently Very Important People opening this very pavilion in 1964. Back then it was all creosoted, white-glossed and square – full of hope and home team advantage. How many shots since then had its skin rebounded – physical blows or cracking echoes? How many spiked dimples pocked its wooden floors? How many slaps from gloves, bats, pads, boxes and curses had its walls absorbed? How much anger, passion, indignation or bonhomie had seeped into its subframe? I could not help wondering how many illicit affairs had been conducted within its covert cladding. Or maybe someone had even been conceived in there, and they now work for Blunt Construction.

24 February

It's happened! I was down in the utility room at seven this morning, attempting to see straight enough to get the milk in my tea. From habit, I checked the temperature inside the propagator – 21 centigrade; a little high, but within prescribed limits. I'd checked the trays last night, and the surfaces of the compost were as flat and uninterrupted as a becalmed sea. I can see the side-mounted thermometer from where I stand, but by virtue of the propagator being on top of the fridge-freezer, I have to clamber onto the washing machine to get a view of the trays. Even though it had been only ten hours or so, I thought I may as well have another look, even though I knew that nothing would have happe—

One. Two, three. Three milky-green skeins, bent double as if conserving heat, were poking out of the tomato tray. I looked closer, and I swear I could see them yawning and rubbing their eyes as they began to stretch their arms out towards the early spring light. I checked the Brunswick onions – still there was nothing, but one solitary, brave needle had punctured the surface of the compost which cossets the Bedfordshire Champions.

I felt as exhilarated as it is possible for me to feel at seven in the morning, but also sensed a strange weight of responsibility descend upon me; something was actually growing, and I have been responsible for the inception of a project whose continuation and subsequent fruition is as much a mystery to me now as parenthood was a decade ago. The fate of these tiny green spears is as daunting and exciting a challenge as that of the successful arrangement of these insignificant letterforms which attempt to describe them.

28 February

At 9.30 p.m. I'm sitting on the loo having just settled the kids down with a combination of Calpol and sharp blows to the temple. Thought I'd write while I was here, as I'm about to have a bath which will, as usual, probably render me as silly and useless as a well-fed dog for the rest of the evening. I wanted to write as the end of today signifies the closure of the winter months. So what happens tomorrow? Does someone in the ether flick the 'spring' switch, and shut down the 'winter' one? I suppose not – tomorrow is just as likely to be colder than today as it is to be warmer, and it is equally possible that there will be hail and/or lightning bolts on the first day of spring as it is that there will be glorious sunshine on the last day of winter.

Still, even if spring doesn't officially start until mid-March, tomorrow does feel like some kind of milestone. Or at least it did until this year. In my memory, all previous winters have simply been months which must be endured as if they were some kind of retribution for having such a good time in the summer. It was a season to be at best tolerated and at worst ignored by means of a duvet, a TV remote control and a diverse scattering of prescription drugs. It seems that previously I have staggered and lurched, blinking, dazed and pale, into spring – wheezing and gasping for light and warmth like a dying smoker clutches for air and another chance. This year, because of an improved understanding of the seasons acquired through gardening, I enter March with, if I may be forgiven, a spring in my step. Why anyone didn't tell me about the healing power of gardening before now I do not know. I feel like shouting it from the shed tops, preaching and evangelizing to all who will listen: THE SALVATION OF SANITY! THE REDEMPTION OF THE SOUL! WITH A SPADE!

17 The Weights We All Carry

A Chosen Burden

2 March

Apart from the odd journal entry while sitting on the toilet, it is just a shade over a week since I last wrote anything related to the plot. Not surprising considering I picked the boys up last Monday and took them to Staffordshire for a few days to visit the family, which firmly precludes any shed-building, greenhouse-glazing or ground-preparing activity, without which there is not a lot to write about.

But I'm home now, and can ignore it no longer. I've been trying to figure out which sex (not gender) gardening is. Intuitively, I would say female, but then I'm a bloke, and I dare say many women would argue that for it to be so stubborn and pedantic, gardening must be male. The reason for this decision is that I like to think of my relationship with gardening as more romantic than platonic. I'm not sure that I could have become quite as emotionally involved with it otherwise. Gardening is not a mate with whom you go out for a beer, a curry and a farting competition, but a coy mistress to be pursued and wooed, loved, nurtured and gently cajoled.

From here, the week ahead looks fit to burst – the plan is to get whatever glass we can into the greenhouse and possibly make some staging to go inside it. I also want to scavenge some panelling from the old pavilion and fix it to the sides of the shed using the nails I bought from the tip last week (about 3 litres of them, 50p). The shed's roof needs felting, its window needs glazing and its door needs a lock in anticipation of there being a good reason for one, i.e. four walls and something within them worth stealing.

In addition to this, there is still digging and ground preparation to be done – this will involve removing anything green and adding plenty of stuff which is brown; compost, fertilizer, rotted grass from the far side of the park and, in the case of the carrot patch, a bag or two of sand to loosen it up and help prevent the carrots from splitting. We also need to start thinking about sowing something at some point. Steve is at work until Thursday, so I've got to crack on on my own.

This list of jobs would have daunted me a year ago, when sometimes the only time I could bring myself to leave the house was to take Charlie out, but tuning in to the frequency of the seasons has made me aware of the possibility that my 'bipolar disorder or manic depression is, in part at least, sensitive to these meteor-ological and chronological fluctuations. My 'ups' seem to coincide, generally speaking, with the onset of spring and can continue into early summer, whereas my bouts of depression seem to have predominantly stolen in like an emotional thief in autumn and winter. Perhaps this mirroring of moods and months is not an illness at all, but simply a condition that we all, to a lesser or greater extent, suffer from: being human. Since we first started to cultivate land as opposed to hunting on it and gathering from it – around the end of the last ice age some 13,000 years ago – we have been enslaved to the seasons. For that length of time, spring has been been so busy that we are by now genetically programmed to accept that, during these three months, we do not even have time to piss. Similarly, atavism insists that come the end of autumn, when all but the most hardy crops are gathered, we instinctively begin to sharpen, clean and hang up our tools, wrap up warm and tinker with stuff. To withdraw.

My version of this, about a year and a half ago, in the absence of any tools to maintain, was to realize that my teaching job, which gave me far too little time to kill and an overwhelming arsenal of weapons from which to choose, was driving me quite literally insane, and I proceeded to hide under the duvet, peeking out only to reassure myself, by way of watching daytime television, that there would always be someone more inane and less interesting than me. Just.

By being involved in, and in touch with, the rhythmic and cyclic nature of the processes of gardening, I am stepping in time with the feet of many millions of ancestors. Perhaps bipolar disorder is simply another name for what happens when we try to ignore this rhythm.

Today we got to the stage where roughly a third of the greenhouse is glazed. Steve and I spent the day slicing short but deep nicks into the pads of our fingers and thumbs, but at least got a result for our efforts, as we did actually manage to cut some glass as well. We are now left with a few large and awkward rhombuses which we are not sure what to do with, but I'll work something out during the week. Not much has happened to the shed since our initial burst of activity – this is largely because we are waiting for the shiplap off the pavilion which, according to the Men Who Rudely Knock Things Down, is going to be rudely knocked down tomorrow. The seeds continue to develop nicely, but there is still much digging to be done on the plot, as well as on the allotment. Right, it's 2.20 a.m. and it feels as if someone has poked me in both eyes with something bristly. I'm off to bed.

3 March

Like most young boys, I idolized my father. It has been so long now since his still somewhat mysterious death (over half my life ago), that it is difficult to remember which of the reasons why I did so were born of reality, and which of idealism. His death remains an enigma to me because, as far as I knew, until he died he simply had bent and swollen joints which looked and sounded mighty painful. There was talk of questionable hospital hygiene and air-conditioning systems, but I think the truth of the matter was that he had been in and out of hospital more times than the laundry truck in the few years before he died, and his body had just had enough. He had become weak, while I still believed him to be strong, and he died less than a handful of years after I had started to call him Dad rather than Daddy.

I guess I looked up to him so much because I saw him as a decent, gentle and honest man and a loving, compassionate father. But what filled me with awestruck reverence more than anything when I was a child was his bunch of keys. It was enormous. One of those jangles of steel and brass which necessitates the use of at least three split rings to accommodate all that clanking. I had always assumed that my father's limping and bent gait was due to his arthritic joints being seized up, but I now have a suspicion it was more to do with all the metal in his pocket.

I would ask him over and again what each one was for, and each time he would go through the litany of 'potting shed, storage shed, garage, back door, front door, side door, my car, yer mother's car, office door . . .' I listened intently as he recited, without hesitation, repetition or deviation, where each of the softly jagged slivers of metal allowed him access to. I loved the mechanical poetry of the words as he breathed them through his beard, and I used to watch his deliberate, gnarled fingers turning each key over as he named it. There must have been twenty-five of them, and he justified the presence of each. This is how I remember it anyway – it is entirely plausible that this childhood memory is similar to that which led me to believe, until alarmingly recently, that fridge-freezers are much shorter now than they used to be. Objects may grow relatively smaller over time, but a glimpse of an unrecoverable memory does nothing but increase in stature.

My obsession with my father's bunch of keys being a sign of manliness has carried over into adulthood, but I cannot help thinking that the poor old sod was weighed down as much by his keys, and the proportional and metaphorical weight of their responsibilities, as he was by his illness. Because of this, I have come to believe that there is a direct link between the number of keys on a keyring and how complicated their owner's life is. The more doors you can open, the greater the responsibility you have, and I am convinced that most people carry too much weight – too many keys, and therefore too much responsibility – around with them. Dead weight. Most people probably have at least one defunct key on their chain, or one more novelty keyring than they need, wearing a slightly bigger hole in their pocket. Too large a hole; and one day all the keys will be gone, including the useful ones.

It is with a degree of trepidation, then, that I have just clicked an extra key onto my collection. Until this evening I had three – one for my car and two for the flat. In addition there is an absurdly heavy keyring I made one day when I found myself with two hours, a half-inch thick piece of brass and a milling machine to spare. There is also a surprisingly useful three-bladed Swiss Army knife and, finally, a piece of hexagonal-section steel bar approximately an inch long by an eighth wide, drilled through one end and attached to the main ring by another, smaller, split pin. I have no idea what it is; I found it on the pavement (a source of much curious treasure) and found its ambiguity beguiling. It rubs against the three keys, the brass fob and the knife as a nod towards all the excess weight I have eschewed over the years.

And now another few grammes of steel, embossed with the words 'Tri-circle China', join the collection, and are possibly the most significant of them all – I was lucky enough to have been given my car by my brother-in-law, and seemed to fall into this flat without any more evaluation involved than 'it's got a roof and some radiators'. This new key, though, is to the shed, which now has four good sides. The window is still unglazed, but despite this deficiency, our big wooden box is now as good as ready to put things in, therefore it was necessary to devise a way of making sure they stay there. This means a lock, and a lock, inevitably, means a key. We could, of course, have opted for a combination lock, but neither Steve nor I can yet swear to being able to remember the code unless it is sprayed onto the outside of the shed door. Besides, we actively chose to possess this key and its extra weight, as it opens a door it was our own responsibility to hang. It's only a small key, though – I don't think it will wear a hole in my pocket, and I very much doubt it will make me walk with a limp.

We have made shelter. I feel as if we should be up there now deflowering a wild animal or spit-roasting a virgin in order to celebrate, but a couple of contemplative beers seem to be doing the trick nicely.

The panelling for the sides came, as planned, from the old pavilion. It was not simply that the wood was still in reasonable condition after three decades of weathering that made me want it for the shed. Nor was it merely the fact that it was free – it was also to do with the notion of continuation; the pavilion had seen the passing of three decades of history and passion, and by recycling its carcass into a shed (another, smaller, refuge from another activity) its story might continue. The guys I had spoken to gave me the impression that I should get there early just in case the lads got carried away with their destructive invective, or lest there was a rush on flaky lengths of shiplap, so I was there at nine o'clock. I thought that *was* early.

By the time I arrived, enough had already been stripped – stacked neatly and mostly unbroken – to clad our entire shed twice over.

'You the guy who wants this wood f'ris shed?' A man – as wide as he was tall – wearing tan safety boots and cupping a roll-up under his bright yellow hat, eyed me with the suspicion of someone who knew a fair bit about building and knocking things down looking at someone else who quite obviously knew bugger all about either.

'Yeah.' I tried to get my tone to approximate 'And I could pick all that up with one hand.' I think, however, it came out more as 'But isn't it awfully grubby?' He wedged the soggy end of his cigarette between his lips, and waggled it up and down as he fixed my gaze and said, 'Just chuck it on there and I'll bring it over for you.'

He motioned to the small copse behind me. Lurking on the edge of it was the cutest, squattest little yellow dump truck I've ever seen – all bent and grimy ochre panels and pristine pistons shining cold silver-blue. He helped me load up more than enough timber to finish the shed, I presumed to ensure that I didn't come back and bother him while he was halfway through telling the pavilion how old and ugly he thought it was in an attempt to make it fall over.

I resisted the temptation to ask for a lift to the shed in the bucket of his truck, and thankfully also managed to avoid telling him that I thought it was the cutest, squattest little yellow dump truck I had ever seen. Instead I walked, with as much of an insouciant swagger as I could muster, to the other side of the park. As the truck was designed more for going slowly up steep hills than rapidly across flat parks, I made it to the other side first. I think I also had the edge because I didn't have to stop to re-light a roll-up on the way over. By the time Dave (just guessing), the truck and the timber had chugged over, it had gone out again. It had probably lasted three days already.

'Where yer buildin' it?' The shed was hidden behind the two 'windbreak' shrubs, which seem to have survived my hacking over the winter.

'Just behind here, ta.'

Dave notched the appropriate lever, and deposited the planks, with an ungracious rattle, as close to the gap in the hedge adjacent to our plot as he could. I thanked him as he swung the truck round in a turning circle smaller than Charlie's and raised his right hand, still clutching a disposable lighter, in acknowledgement. He chugged his way back over to the pavilion, the cute little truck belching diesel fumes in an echo of my own gastrointestinal difficulties (there are some things that you shouldn't do the morning after a hot curry and a four pack – lifting, dragging and throwing heavy things are three of them).

As I was knocking the recycled nails through the cedar walls into the framework, the men and machines efficiently and seemingly effortlessly continued to pulverize the pavilion. Ted arrived, suitably equipped with a large bowsaw and a surprisingly ruthless look in his eye. A few others joined the spectacle, gawping onlookers and potential scavengers, circling around the splinters like so many crows.

But this wood was not carrion – dead and rotting; it was being given new life. Barely a fraction of it, perhaps, but it is only necessary to sow a fraction of a sunflower for a plant 10 feet tall. It may be a small amount, and it may just be the sides of our shed, but the fact that the shed now has four solid walls means that we will be able to work our land more easily, and in greater comfort. Luckily, on one of the lengths of wood I had scrounged, someone had sprayed their graffiti tag as the pavilion had sagged into disuse. I made sure that I included this scrawl when cutting the wood for the shed as I figured that its inclusion, if read phonetically, would leave little room for ambiguity on this subject of continuity. The graffiti artist's tag read 'Saime'.

As I hammered, I thought I could hear the pistol-crack echoes of my blows relaying around the park. But when I paused, and the echo did not, I realized that these snaps were in fact originating from the site of the old pavilion, as the last of its trusses succumbed reluctantly and angrily to the licking tongues of 20-foot flames. As I made fast our shed its provenance was – quite literally – spitting fire.

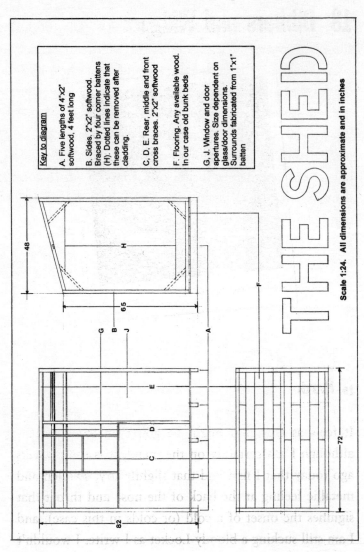

THE SHED

Scale 1:24. All dimensions are approximate and in inches

48

65

72

82

G

B

J

H

E

D

C

A

F

18 Dibbers and Widgers

Go Get 'em Dirty

10 March

It feels as though I might be going on about it but, although I am certainly on the mend, it is three weeks ago today that I first had that slightly dry, swollen and metallic feeling at the back of the nose and throat that signifies the onset of a cold (or colds in this case), and I am still sucking a bloody Locket as I write. I wouldn't mind as much if I could tell what flavour it is. On the way home on Saturday I bought some compost which I put in the boot along with all my good intentions of performing emergency onion transplants – having seemed to come through without a hitch, over the last few days they have begun to look decidedly unwell. However, I think I must have actually put the compost *on top* of the good intentions because when I got home, I couldn't find them anywhere.

Instead, having experienced something of a relapse, I ensconced myself on the sofa and watched the rugby, marvelling at how it is possible for people to be capable of running without coughing or indeed able to stand unaided for longer than ten minutes. And it is odd how physical illness not only saps the ability to lift a gardening tool, but also the motivation to lift a pen and do anything useful with it. I've jotted the odd thing down in my journal but, without looking, I have a horrible feeling that I've written an awful lot about how little I have written.

The onions really weren't looking too healthy. In fact they were looking decidedly consumptive – they'd gone from grids of thrusting little green fingers to sagging strands of anaemic yellow string flopping about on the black loam like tiny dead elvers. Through a combination of common sense, talking to people and leafing through books I concluded that one or more of three things had happened. First, they had run out of legroom because I had sown them in trays, not the pots recommended on the packets. Secondly, they may not be getting enough light. The third possibility is that they have come out in sympathy with me, because they sure as hell look like I've been feeling.

I decided on a belt-and-braces approach, as I reckoned this would probably be quicker than trying to pinpoint exactly what the problem was, so yesterday I pricked out six of the pluckier onions into amply deep pots, and placed them on the south-facing window sill in my bedroom.

So, the last forty-eight hours have been the first for a while during which plot digging has been even a vaguely viable option. Unfortunately Saturday saw Steve stricken with the same bug, so while I have been irritatingly perky and full of that energy which comes from believing, finally, that you are not going to die imminently, Steve has been sliding down the slope which leads to believing that dying imminently would be just fine. Still, we did get bed 'f' (possibly peas, possibly sweetcorn) dug over yesterday – again a question of removing forlorn and flapping pieces of turf, weeds and large rocks. We had overturned this section three or four months ago and, by yesterday, the grass had not rotted sufficiently for us to dig it into the soil, but had decayed just enough to ensure that it fell apart when we tried to lift it with our forks and hurl it into the 'barrow.

We had dug for about half an hour when Steve, as white as the inside of a freshly cut leek, declared that if he had to do any more exercise than it took to walk home and drink Lemsip then he was going to either die, or be sick or possibly both. Because I was now He-man, I could afford to be magnanimous. I assured him that after the three weeks I'd had, I fully understood and he should go home immediately and proceed to take all and any available drugs. I told him that he had done much more already than I had when I had been feeling so lousy, and he must not run the risk of turning what was, after all, only a minor cold into something far more ominous. I watched him stumble and stagger up the path by the side of the plots, and just as his trembling hand was reaching for the bolt to release the 'squeak-ding' gate, I could resist it no longer.

'Lightweight! Pussy! Big Girl's Pants!'

I knew that he would not be able to summon the voice or the energy to shout back, but I was certainly expecting a finger or two, or possibly a hand movement suggesting that I should go and milk a cow rapidly. But no, Steve could not even bring himself to respond to my insults in gestures – usually something he does gladly. He really must be ill.

I mixed some of the cricket-square grass into the aerated soil, along with a bag of soil conditioner from the tip, using the three-pronged tool which belonged to my father. I have no idea what this tool is called, and I do not care. It has a head which must weigh a couple of pounds fitted to a hardwood handle, six feet long, and an inch and a half wide, which I would like to say is hornbeam or American mountain ash, but is probably beech or something equally ordinary. My father was incapable of holding this tool without uttering phrases such as 'don't make 'em like they used to' and 'tools like this do all the work for you. Lovely, see that?' It was as if that handle were impregnated with a balm which imbued the user with Essence of Sentimental Old Fart. The head is made from what is obviously good quality steel – hard enough to withstand the continual abrasion and collision of soil and stones, yet tough enough to allow sufficient flexibility for it to bend instead of break. Use the same grade of steel for a pair of scissors and you may as well cut with your fingers. Use a high carbon steel (as used in blades) for a three-pronged gardening tool and it would shatter upon impact with the first rock. My dad would have known about this also, and I cannot help but think that it is the duty of all fathers to be able to witter on shallowly at their children about a wide variety of subjects, in much the same way that a father isn't a proper father until he has an assortment of old tobacco tins or jam-jars full of nails, screws and washers, or until he knows all ten ways of being out in cricket.

The bed looked fantastic after I'd finished and it struck me that it's possible to describe good soil in the same way as expensive plain chocolate – rich, dark and complex. It is possible to smell as well as see when a soil is good, especially in spring rain. Picking up a handful and squeezing it in your palm or breaking it with your fingers is also a good indicator of clay, sand or something in between. You can hear it being sliced by a spade when it is not too stoney, and I'm not sure whether I dreamed this or not, but I think I read somewhere that some people can actually gauge the quality and type of a soil sample by tasting it. I sincerely hope this is true, as I feel that the world is just a little more interesting if there are people in it who lick soil. I would also be mighty worried if I had started dreaming about people who do.

On a scientific level, I'd be hard pressed to differentiate between good soil and a pile of sheep-shit, but I can kind of sense when it's right. The stuff we dug over yesterday had an air of boredom and meanness about it, and as if it could do with a bit of motivation. Having done the work we did, it now seems to have a new sense of purpose – possibly even that of sustaining edible plants.

This afternoon, I spent a very happy hour or so in the 'garden' pricking out my tomatoes and what was left of the salvageable onions. The tomatoes were beginning to look a little cramped in the propagator, like a kitchen full of swaying, drunken adolescents at a house party. I took them all outside along with two window-sill trays and thirty or so three-inch pots. I placed them on the square slab of concrete in the 'garden' and retrieved my folding stool and a sack of compost from the shed. Sitting on the stool, I arranged the rest of the equipment in front of me, whereupon I stood up again, searching for the knife I had used as a makeshift widger for the first of the onions. A widger, apparently, is the tool used for levering out seedlings from tray to pot or bed. However, it must have slipped into a parallel universe, as I couldn't find it anywhere. At least I couldn't find it in all the really obvious places I could think of and I wasn't going to look in too many more as there was a drawer full of widgers in the kitchen. Just as I was heading from the 'garden' to the flat to get one of them, it dawned on me that I had five perfectly serviceable widgers, not to mention dibbers (or dobbers or nobbers) sticking out from the palm of each hand. A great deal of the pleasure of gardening, for me, is derived from the inherently tactile nature of many of its processes, and to obfuscate this pleasure by the use of more tools than is strictly necessary is to miss out on one-fifth of gardening. To refute that there is an abstract, but nonetheless tangible, thrill to be had from running your hands through a tray of compost – breaking up some of the larger clumps by squeezing and rubbing them in your fingers – is tantamount to saying that there is no more to gardening than a simple sequence of mundane, repetitive and laborious tasks.

I have a gardening catalogue in front of me, advertising a dibber and widger set: 'Make holes with the dibber and gently lift the seedlings with the widger – only £1.50 per set.' Amazing that many millennia of evolution have given us, if we are lucky, two opposable thumbs and eight harmonious fingers and some people are still willing to spend money on a tool which makes a hole roughly the diameter of, well, a finger. I am aware that until comparatively recently I was using a cotton bud to sow onions with (but then I was also using a ruler to measure out the holes and tweezers to drop the seeds into them) but, considering the current state of the onions, I may as well have thrown them on the drive and spat on them.

After the fun I had this afternoon widging with my right and dibbing with my left, I can only implore anyone who is thinking of buying this pair of tools, which will undoubtedly end up in a kitchen drawer with an odd length of string and two rusty drawing pins, to go and buy a gardening book for £1.50 from your local charity shop and smudge its pages with your soiled fingers.

Including the half-dozen I potted yesterday, there are now eleven onions seedlings and eighteen juvenile tomato plants wedged into their very own individual pots, placed in two long, thin trays on my bedroom window sill. They are in warm, rich and moist compost and will be exposed to as much light as they are going to get in this flat. The onions are still looking pathetic, although post-cold, post-winter positive thinking tells me that some of the feistier ones from yesterday have, like spring steel, started to find their memory and lurch upwards once more. This is, frankly, more than I was expecting of them. Not as much, however, as I'd hoped for from the tomatoes. When I pricked them out earlier, their 2–3 inch stems had described gentle, smooth, S-shaped curves as a result of their tray being turned occasionally to vary their aspect. Now they look as if they are doing nothing as much as sulking, and I feel like the square dad in the company car who did indeed arrive cringingly early to break up the house party. Whereas before they were all in the same nice, warm house and generally having a cosy old get-together, they are now separated like a class of naughty pupils forbidden to talk to one another. But I know best – they are never going to grow up and put down their own roots if they slouch around with their mates for the rest of their lives. As if in unanimous protest, they have all decided to redraw themselves from sinuous, sweeping Ss to tight – sometimes even coiled – hairpins. Most of their heads are lolling spinelessly and have touched down on the pillow of compost beneath them. If I put my good ear close enough, I can hear them mumbling 'I hate you' and 'I didn't ask to be sown'. I am hoping that this is just a reaction to the shock of being yanked from where they were quite comfortable, thank you very much, to a new and strange place. It's either that or the possibility that human skin secretions are deadly to tomato seedlings, and I should have used a dibber, and possibly even a widger, after all.

19 Circles, Sets and Odd Events

I Wouldn't Do it Like That

11 March

The mornings have developed a pleasant rhythm over the last couple of weeks or so. I usually wake between eight and nine and down at least two mugs of tea before I piece together what month it is and deem myself sufficiently safe and sighted to operate the toaster and a knife. Suitably refreshed, but often with at least one burnt or lacerated digit, I proceed to check on the

progress or otherwise of the seedlings, along with whatever else is potted up or planted out in the 'garden'
(garlic, six raspberry canes and a couple of pots of
sunflowers and nasturtiums that the boys and I sowed
a couple of weekends ago). Most of them seem to be
doing one of two things – very well or bugger all. I do
not object to either. 'Very well' (garlic shooting and
piercing the air with deafening greenness, flowers ger-
minating and sending forth exploratory paired leaves,
tomatoes, even since yesterday, attempting to defy gravity and hold their heads up straight) is obviously preferable, but even the 'bugger all' of the raspberries does
not concern me just yet. I've had enough experience of
their cousin the blackberry in another part of the 'garden' to lead me to believe that it won't be long before I
am exasperated at my inability to *stop* them growing.
But the onions, and I realize that this is going to sound
impatient and petulant, are really starting to piss me off.
I wouldn't mind so much if they had the decency to just
collapse, blanch and die on me. At least then I could use
the pots and compost for something more compliant.
As with the tomatoes yesterday, I want to give them a
good talking-to about all the other onions in the world
who are worse off than they are, and remind them of
all the warmth, shelter and food I have lavished upon
them. Despite the fact that this lecture would probably

actually have more effect on the onions than it does on the average teenager, I still think I would be wasting my breath, but I am now at a loss as to what else I can do. The more books I read, and the more the onions refuse to stand up straight, the more I am coming over to Christopher Lloyd's way of thinking. In an attempt to intimidate them into pulling their socks up ('socks which I clean, and don't you forget it') I read this to them earlier on from *Gardener Cook*:

> *I see little point in the home-grown onion. Those on sale are as good and may have better keeping qualities, having been grown where summers are warmer and more ripening. Your own crop is expected to last 6 or 9 months and there will be many losses along the way. Buying them, 1 kg or 2 lb at a time, they have little scope for rotting.*[3]

Many losses along the way? I'm not sure he meant this many, so balls to the sulky little sods. I'd planned to try potting up some more but I'm not sure I can be bothered now. I'll see if I can get anything from the ones I've potted up so far, but as for the rest of them – tonight they sleep with the earthworms. The spaces in my propagator, my compost and my day would be better filled with something a little more grateful.

3 *Gardener Cook*, Christopher Lloyd, Frances Lincoln, 1997.

13 March

At the plot, breaking off from re-digging the last bed in readiness for planting (bed 'e', which used to have some productive currant bushes in it). Two more rows of digging and removing ever thinning turfs, and we will be ready. When Steve and I were here recently, we found ourselves jubilantly concurring that once this bed is dug, that will be 'it', meaning that we will in a sense have 'finished' something. In many ways, we were right – once we had squared this oblong and made it brown, we would have completed a certain phase. But the conversation served only to highlight the fact that gardening is the ultimate activity for the confirmed rainbow chaser. If we removed every root, spore and seed from each of the beds, it would be only a short amount of time before more arrived to take their place – blown here by the wind or carried by humans and other animals. Besides, this 'finishing' simply allows us to then 'begin' something else. Gardening has not a great deal to do with the domination of nature, but is more concerned with striking a delicate balance between controlling it, and allowing it to answer back.

Right, I'm going to get on and get this bed 'finished'. Then, for the first time since taking on a barren patch of weed-infested and undernourished-looking soil nearly six months ago, we will be able to assert reasonably confidently that all the beds are ready to grow more than dandelions and couch grass.

23 March

I have done very little at or about the plot recently. The reasons for this are two types of parental responsibility: first, that which dictates that I am responsible for the care of my two children, and secondly that which requires my mother to take the youngest of hers on holiday to West Cornwall with a view to visiting gardens, beaches, galleries and cream-tea shops. I had my kids for a few days and then went on holiday with Mum.

So, with all the beds more or less ready, it's now time to start planting something in them. Onions are back on the menu for when we get round to doing so. My puny little seedlings, despite Steve's assurance that he gave them a good talking-to while I was away, don't seem to have got any more cooperative. There are five which look as if they might actually make it at least to the salad stage, but five out of the seventy that I sowed regimentally a few weeks ago is hardly a good strike rate – not bad in terms of decent photos from a couple of rolls of film, but lousy for two trays of onions. Certainly not enough to manufacture a couple of robust and bulging 'ropes' for late-summer photos which, since reading *Gardener Cook*, are the only reason I'm bothered about growing onions anyway. To this end, and due to me laying on my sense of loss as thick and bittersweet as molasses, Mum has very kindly furnished us with a few pounds of onion sets. I had wanted to grow them from seed mainly because, I think, this made life perversely difficult for me – a speciality of mine when things get dull. I've masked this by waffling on about an increased involvement with the life cycle leading to a greater empathy with the universe or something like that. It's all balls – I just get bored when life gets too easy.

I also wanted to grow onions from seed because I wanted to tell people that I had, which is just about the lamest justification for doing anything. So we are growing onions from sets because that is now the only way we stand even a cat against Charlie's chance of growing any at all, and this plot has taught me enough by now for me not to care who knows where my onions came from, and that life is quite capable of being difficult on its own, so why should I give it any assistance?

More pressing than 'how?' right now, though, is 'how

many?' We have 80 whites – Sturon, I think they are called, and 57 Red Barons. I like these names; there is something abstractly reliable about the former, and the latter has an inevitable air of dashing, devil-may-care about it. Not qualities I'd ever associated with onions before, but gardening really is, it seems, full of surprises. Apparently, onion sets should be planted 5 inches apart. By my calculations that means we have about 680 inches of onions jostling and tessellating in those bags, or roughly 57 feet. The onion plot is 9 feet 6 inches × 14 feet, so if we plant them parallel to the short edge, we will end up with 6 rows; just about right if we interplant them with carrots as planned and not a bad guess seeing that my decision regarding quantity was based on something roughly halfway between 'quite obviously not enough' and 'taking the piss considering I'm not paying for them'.

I felt that we should be extra-fussy about the carrot and onion bed with particular regard to stones, weeds and other extraneous vegetation. However, we are not going to be digging in any compost or similar additives, as carrots thrive in a rich soil. This may sound like a positive thing only to be encouraged, but carrots are so partial to a nutrient-laden soil that the roots will go looking for these goodies like kids seeking sweets on a treasure hunt. And carrots, like kids, soon discover that the best way to find something is to split up. Not that I have any real objection to forked or otherwise humorous carrots – I assume they taste the same as straight ones, though I guess the latter are easier to clean – but we've got 'laang, straight and reliable' Autumn Kings to do justice to, and I'm taking no chances with our carrots or anything else when it comes to that stick. And what would be the point of growing a carrot 'because it looks like the ones that Bugs Bunny eats' if it's going to end up looking like the John Merrick of the vegetable world? So, in view of the fact that onion sets aren't that fussy about soil quality either (unlike seeds, which evidently need Waitrose hand-selected and hand-crumbled compost, humidity and temperature controls and hand-feeding by scantily clad servants), I reckon that the onions and carrots will get along just fine in there.

As I wandered home earlier, having briefly reacquainted myself with the plot and watched Charlie turn the half-mile or so walk around the park into a three-mile run, I caught sight of something which at once repelled and fascinated me. A sight so rare, incomprehensible and disturbing as to make me question my every assumption regarding the nature of time, logic or reality. I think in fact it was Charlie who spotted it first, almost preternaturally. His hackles bristled like iron filings under a magnet as he uncharacteristically pulled back his upper lip and uttered a deep, feral growl. Trembling, I restrained him on the shortest of leads as the full shock and implication of what we saw hit me.

It was Ken.

Doing some gardening.

You hear stories of moments like this: a keen amateur photographer just happens to be in the right place at the right time, when something quite remarkable and entirely unprecedented occurs, and he is lucky enough to record it on film. Henceforth, I would be known in hushed tones throughout the allotment community as the 'Guy Who Caught Ken Gardening'.

20 Pre-vegetable Tension

Exactly what it says on the Tube

28 March

At some point I was going to pause for a while to reflect on the plot's immediate past, before Steve and I first sank our forks into it, in order to pay some kind of tribute to the elderly lady who tended this allotment when it was not even a twinkle in our beery eyes. However, in view of how much of a pain in the backside the last hour or so has been I am now more inclined to say balls to the silly old trout for seeing fit to fill the bloody place with flowers. Not benign and convenient annuals which leave no trace of themselves save for a bit of compost fodder. Oh no, she had to put in about three billion bloody bulbs, didn't she? I have no idea what they are, and no desire to find out. Nor am I going to keep them and put them somewhere else. I am going to continue to throw them, with ever increasing force, into the orange bucket and then dump them unceremoniously on top of the pile of turfs next to the shed, where they will probably grow quite happily in the way that unwanted plants do when they are abused and ignored. Put 'em in rows in lovely rich compost and they will probably wilt and die. Stuff them into a crack in a wall and you're well away.

What I find quite staggering is the fact that we have already done this bed at least once and still there are millions of these things. It's not as if the carrots aren't quite demanding enough already with their 'Ooh, don't like big stones' and 'Soil? Oh, not too rich because it makes me split but not too poor otherwise I just won't grow' in their silly, sing-song orange voice. Little brats. Only 30p a bag in Tesco's, and don't you bloody forget it, you fussy orange bastards.

Allotments are for food, not for growing bloody crocuses or whatever they are. Growing flowers as companions for vegetables is to be positively encouraged; most marigolds, apparently, have the ability to make virtually all vegetables bomb-proof, as well as increasing their IQ by at least ten points and making them generally more pleasant and considerate. But there should be some law preventing daft old biddies from sitting around their allotment pretending that they are in an English Country Garden. Of course I realize that, technically, this is exactly where they are, but the fallout which settled around the General Inclosure Act of 1845 did not include, to my knowledge, the indignation of the common man at being deprived of his right to grow delphiniums.

Right, I have become aware of the possibility that I am only going on about flowers in an attempt to avoid digging the bloody things up.

A little later. I think I got them all. Actually, that is a lie – I am quite sure that I got nowhere near all of them, but I unearthed an amount sufficient to make me feel that I deserved a break. I figure that we can pull the rest out when they dare show their face, looking suspiciously straight-leaved and un-carrot-like.

Wednesday morning saw Steve and me at the plot together for the first time in what seemed like weeks.

This, though, was something of an auspicious occasion. That day, all the peripheral activities (digging, making sheds and compost bins, talking drivel, etc.) surrounding and supporting our very purpose for being there were to be put aside to make way for the activity that would finally and truly bestow 'gardener' status on us. That day, we were going to perform the absolutely vital, but still faintly ludicrous, task of sowing some seeds. The propagator experience had not prepared me for this at all – not only had half of what I put in there died, but also the plot seemed so big and surrounded by so much air and space. And all that rough, bullying soil.

But all we had done there for what is now six months had been, directly or indirectly, in preparation for doing just this; we had cleared the best part of 1,500 square feet of land of its various undesired materials – weeds, grasses, bulbs, stones, perilous metal, grubs and anything else which looked as if it might be a threat to our soup ingredients and had added what will hopefully be enough substances to encourage them to flourish. And there we were, having been such brave, manly and purposeful frontiersmen, terrified at the prospect of doing something whose outcome could be quantified and judged. It was possible to get this bit wrong. Not easily, true; but for Steve and me, not an entirely unlikely eventuality.

ALLOTTED TIME

Steve seemed to be labouring, as he often does, under the touching but wildly erroneous assumption that I had a better idea of what I was doing than he did. I think I just happen to be better than he is at bluffing with an air of authority. There is, of course, an element of false modesty at work here – I have in fact spent a bit of time doing some research into each of our crop's requirements. Which means that I've read the backs of the seed packets from across the table while Stevie was looking at the pictures on the front. We convinced ourselves that this would get us through any eventuality. I had a rough idea of what to do with the seeds, and Steve knew what they looked like when they had grown.

But there was no 'when' – only a hesitant and timorous 'if'. At the time, our trepidation seemed a little silly, and we tried to cover it up by swearing a lot and speaking in monosyllabic grunts while adjusting our underwear and its contents. On reflection, though, I feel that there was some justification for our concerns. The plot has become, to us, an entity which represents much more than the sum of its parts. We have invested far more than calloused hands, compost and throbbing lumbar regions in this plot; we have imbued it with our own peculiar brand of faith – a faith not only in the reliability of nature, but also in ourselves and in the security of our place in the life cycle. Eventually, we decided that we would deem vegetables which refused to grow in soil which had received that sort of treatment so churlish as to be inedible anyway, so we forged ahead.

We would do a few rows each of carrots and onions and, considering our reservations regarding the former's seed getting lost because the soil was just too big, did a row of onions first. Our confidence needed all the help it could get, and was simply not inspired by the fact that the carrot seeds couldn't even manage a rattle when you shook the packet but instead only mustered a limp, diaphanous 'swish'. Onion sets are large enough to juggle with, and their tops would still be poking out after planting so we could check that no one had stolen, eaten or moved them when we had finished. This may sound paranoid, but we were still smarting from when some bugger nicked our picnic table.

Even so, we still felt a little like children planting coins in expectation of a cash-crop as we stretched our line exactly parallel to the edge of the bed and ceremonially drew a narrow drill – each of us cutting half the bed from the middle to our respective sides using the thick, heavy draw-hoe that I bought from the tip for a pound. We drew the drill just deep enough to allow the pointy, papery onion tops to stand proud above the surface, having of course first been cosseted in sifted compost. This addition of compost was not based on any kind of research or hard facts – it just felt like the right thing to do, like feeding vegetables to a child. Besides, we knew just how crap the rest of the soil was, and even though neither crop is particularly soil-sensitive, we still figured that they might need a bit of a head start. I measured and broke a couple of sticks to the prescribed five inches, tossed one of them to Steve, and we worked our way from each side to the middle, adjusting the spacing of the last ones so as to leave a neat, regular line of orange-beige dots like a row of full stops in an earthy text.

From the black bucket I fished one of my home-made plant labels, fashioned from a cut, washed and flattened (the back of a spoon's the best way, mind your fingers) tomato puree tube. Placing it on the shed floor, I embossed it with 'Sturon 26 March' using an old ball-point pen, and tied it loosely with green flax twine to one of the bamboo canes (job lot from the tip, another pound) which Steve had sunk at either end. I figured that if it was left to flap around a bit, the metallic shimmer and clatter might scare birds away, as well as reminding us what we had planted there shortly before they all died. We agreed that we were now gardeners, despite the fact that planting our first row of twenty or so onions had taken us the best part of three-quarters of an hour. We needed coffee before we could even think about carrots.

We had been correct in our assumption that doing onions first would embolden us sufficiently to believe that the carrots were worth doing and may not actually be a practical joke on behalf of Mr Sutton himself. We gave them the same loving care that we had bestowed on the onions, noting that sowing St Valerys in anything stronger than a gentle breeze is inadvisable, and even then they should be sown only when in the lee of a stout wall. After we had interred them under 12.7 mm of compost and soil, we reverently creaked to our feet, and Steve summed up poignantly and succinctly what both of us were feeling at this truly pivotal moment: 'Well, that's fucked that up, then.'

We put in another row of onions (reds this time) and one of Autumn King to appease the Stick of Ken. We surveyed the results of our efforts – which visibly amounted to eight sticks and just over three dozen incongruously coloured dots, and reminded ourselves of two things. First, that there is always much more happening underneath than is immediately visible on the surface, and secondly, that they were all going to be dead within a week, so it didn't really matter anyway.

We both stole self-satisfied glances at what was now very definitely our plot. Not only had we removed a few hundred pounds of unsolicited plants, but we had also put some decidedly intentional ones, very neatly, in their place. I'm still unsure whether this meant we had started or finished or – more likely – both, but one thing was for sure – we had made our mark, or marks; most of them punctuation.

Not, as it turned out, as much of a mark as some inconsiderate and ignorant sod's dog had made before I returned yesterday morning. At first I didn't notice the two fairly sizeable indentations, probably due to a combination of denial and the fact that it was still early enough to make placing one foot in front of the other hazardous enough without the additional complication of checking for the paw prints of anything else. I eventually got together all the equipment necessary to plant another row or two of onions and carrots. This naturally took me a couple of attempts, and at one point I did actually try to start without the bags of onions. Just as I had stretched the line from one side of the bed to the other, thinking about how much easier this job is with two people involved, and was walking to Ted's plot to borrow his enormous scaffold plank to place across the bed, I noticed that someone's bloody dog had seen fit to run straight over it. Where, only the day before, there had been perfect, raked and firmed flatness there was now a brace of craters, dry-rimmed and damp-bowled. As luck would have it, both the paw prints had fallen neatly between the rows we had planted the day before, but this was hardly the point, and most certainly more through accident than design.

But, alongside my ire, this intrusion made me feel somehow proud, as it put me in mind of the moment the previous day, as we were sowing our first row of carrots, when I needed to stretch a little to reach the middle of the row (Ted had watched us doing this and told us about his plank then). I thought that it would do no harm to gently place my right knee on the bed between the current row and the hypothetical next one. Little did I know what a fine job we had made of digging, sifting and raking this bed to the fine tilth required by fussy, straight carrots. It was similar in texture to the very best deep, damp sand – at once springy and sponge-like as well as accepting and enveloping. When I had finished scattering and waving a final goodbye to the tiny seeds, I realized that I didn't really want to remove my knee from the earth which was moulded snugly and warmly around it. This was quickly followed by the realization that my knee had, in fact, plunged so far into the soil that I could not remove it without assuming a position more usually associated with a yoga manual or the Kama Sutra.

I wouldn't have minded this canine transgression so much if I had thought that the dog in question had appreciated the experience of plunging its padded paws into such exquisite soil, but my suspicions already lay with one of a pair of springer spaniels (mainly because I had seen them walking home from the park on the way up). In my experience, most pet (as opposed to working) springers don't generally have sufficient brains to remember what they are doing halfway through retrieving a stick, so the likelihood of them having sufficient capacity to pause a moment to savour the aesthetic qualities, let alone the psycho-sexual implications, of plunging their pads into fine, soft, warm, moist and forgiving soil, is slim in the extreme.

I was furious, though. This was far more than a couple of paw prints in the soil; this was a flagrant disregard of the effort involved in our getting to this stage, and displayed an ignorance not only of the practicalities, but also of the philosophies of gardening. It was nothing less than a violation of my rights to work this piece of land as laid down in the Smallholdings and Allotments Acts and Amendments of 1887, 1890, 1908, 1922, 1925 and 1950. Although I'll let him off the Land Settlement Facilities Act of 1919, as this applied only to returning servicemen and did not, as far as I can ascertain, mention spaniels. This transgression was, in short, nothing less than sweeping up my dreams into a pile and spitting on them. Or that's how it felt. It was as if, after Steve and I had meticulously punctuated our double-spaced plot on Wednesday, sometime between then and yesterday morning some bloody dog had come along and written 'this is all bollocks' in the margin. I entertained notions of cordoning off the prints and taking plaster casts of them with the intention of comparing them with any likely looking suspects (brown and white, floppy ears, stupid) and, upon finding the culprits, dragging them back to the plot, stuffing their noses into the holes and yelling, 'Did you do that?' I would then impose some kind of canine community service – digging, perhaps, or a few hours of accompanying Charlie (mentally not so much challenged as defeated) on a spot of imaginary cat chasing.

When Steve arrived, I mustered up as much indignation as I had left and showed him, with expletives and gesticulating arms, the crevasses (in my mind they were getting bigger by the minute).

'That's a bit of a bugger,' he said as he bent down and smoothed over the evidence with his hands. 'Still, it's only a couple of paw prints in the soil, and at least they're not on the rows.'

He had a point, and besides, I wasn't going to get my plaster casts now, was I? We planted more onions and carrots.

I left to collect the boys from school, then drove us back up to the park again to kick the dog and throw sticks for the football. Before we did, I marched the children to the plot and told them that if they wanted to eat then they had better look at all the work we had done and make noises which suggested that they were both impressed and interested. The most convincing would get extra chocolate biscuits for pudding. My two children are remarkable in many ways, and few more so than in their ability to sound genuinely proud of their old man for pushing some sticks into the soil if it means they get extra chocolate. As it happens, over the last few years they have seen their old man in some states which may well have precluded my pushing any sticks into the soil, so I guess that it is nice for them to see me being so productive. I promised them that if they were good, and didn't eat too many chocolate biscuits, then we could come here over the weekend and push some sticks into their soil as well. When they said, 'Cool!' I told them that they could stop sounding fascinated because there was no further sugary enticement in the offing, but they really did seem enthusiastic at the prospect. So much so that I had to drag them away from the plot by their hair (which I have been encouraging them to grow for this very purpose) towards the park.

I have lived here for a year and a half now. I mention this in the context of the fact that for me to do anything consistently for anything more than twelve months (holding down a job, being married, etc.) is something worth remarking on in itself. I would like to say that this is down to my being a wild and restless free spirit who tiptoes through life lightly, but I suspect that it is because as soon as the pile of washing-up (literal or emotional) gets too high, I have always tended to think that it is easier to simply move on than to clean it. This tendency grew more and more disturbing and frustrating not only for me, but also for those around me (many of whom have done a good deal of tidying up after me) until a couple of years ago. After a few well-intentioned but inaccurate diagnostic stabs in the dark, it was finally recognized that I was (and probably had been for some time) suffering from manic depression. Mental health problems, like so many others, are much easier to carry when you have a handle on them.

Before I moved here I had, on average over the previous fifteen years or so, moved house roughly every six months, and the longest I ever held down a job – as a college lecturer – was seventeen months. When I resigned, I received a letter from the principal which started with the line 'I am sorry you are leaving after such a short time.' In comparison, then, I now feel I am a part of the Twyford establishment, and a large part of feeling settled in this community has been due, I'm sure, to the existence of the dog-walking sector. Because of this, I have noticed a peculiar dog-owners' trait: that we all learn the names of each other's dogs before we bother to ask the name of the owner. I suspect that this is because when we throw sticks or hit tennis balls for our dogs, we say something along the lines of 'Go on, Charlie – fetch!' But, if and when the dog returns (more if than when with Charlie), he doesn't drop it and say, 'There you go, Robin!' I was recently greeted, by a newly acquainted fellow dog walker, as the 'Lurcher Man'. I secretly glowed, partly with pride, but mainly out of relief at having not been called the 'Arse-dog Man.' The conversation continued along the regular lines:

'What's his name?'

'Charlie.'

The next thing everyone says is:

'Isn't he lovely!'

'No, he's an arse.'

'Look! He's got blue eyes!'

'Well I never, so he has!'

'Hasn't he got unusual markings!'

'No, he hasn't. My children painted him.'

After a time, I stopped being the 'Lurcher Man' and became 'Charlie's Dad', which is surely an indictment of either Charlie's Mum or of my sexual proclivities. Similarly I have got to know Dukie and Dukie's Dad, Rachel and her Mum and Dad, Bunty and Bunty's Mum and Dad, as well as a few others.

Yesterday, though, something quite remarkable happened. I learned that the Beagle Lady's name is Chris before I learned what the Beagle Lady's beagles were called. An anomaly indeed. Well, not quite an anomaly, because I was told this by Mick, whose dog's name I do not know either – mainly because I suspect that Mick's black labrador actually died some years ago, whereupon he had it stuffed and mounted on wheels, like a child's pull-along toy. Throw a stick for that one and you'd have to give it a bloody big push to stand even half a chance of getting it back. As I was rabidly ranting to Mick about the canine trespass incident earlier on (I knew it wasn't his dog as there had been no tyre tracks), he told me that I should speak to Chris about it, as she was the parish council representative for the prevention of dogs running over carrot seeds. I didn't recognize the name.

'You know, the Beagle Lady.'

Of course. And remarkably enough, there she was after the boys and I had done a circuit of the park and Mick had dragged his squeaking and trundling hound back home for a spot of WD40. As the boys and I approached her, I tried not to swagger with the gait of a man who had information which she did not. I knew her name. Ha! And I knew that someone's dog had trampled on our plot earlier. I could sense that she was already on the back foot.

'Hi, Robin – heard you had some dog trouble on the allotment earlier.'

The quieter the village, the more deafening the roll of the jungle drum. It transpired that the gap in the fence next to our plot, which allowed said incursion to happen, harks back to the days when the allotments used to stretch right over to the other side of the park, and was part of the main thoroughfare which cut right through the middle of them (in 1911, there were seven acres of allotment gardens in Twyford; now there is a shade under one acre and slightly more than six acres of Tesco's just down the M3, which neatly and hideously bisects Twyford Down). Apparently, if that right of way is blocked then all of the parish councillors will turn into newts, or something like that. I may have missed some of the detail there, as I stopped listening as soon as she told me I wasn't allowed to shoot any and all dogs which came within a hundred yards of the plot.

Chris did, however, very kindly say that she would raise the matter at the next sub-committee meeting, which happened to be taking place later yesterday evening, in order to get the ball rolling. I suggested a large stone one between the two fence-posts. She also said that she would mention it at the next parish council meeting proper.

'But you know what parish councils are like, so I wouldn't hold your breath.'

She also assured me that if I wanted to put something up as a temporary barrier in the meantime, then she couldn't really see a problem as most parish councillors are newts at the weekend anyway. She had been really very sympathetic, understanding and good-humoured about the whole thing, but I couldn't help wondering two things. First, I assumed by her comment about me not holding my breath that she meant that councillors are very busy people, and it is quite feasible that this is so. But how busy do you have to be to preclude the phoning of a Gate Expert, telling them you want a gate, where you want it and how much will that cost, please? Secondly, do I really look like someone who knows what parish councils are like?

Speaking of things parochial, I feel that I should

mention our local magazine, the very slim and therefore appositely entitled *What's On in and Around Twyford*, which drops through my letter box every month. The first time it came, I took it to be a questionnaire from someone at the end of their social tether. Upon closer inspection, however, this pamphlet regularly contains enough information to make even the most hardcore of thrill seekers quiver with trepidation. The one which caught my eye most inexorably this month was an event being staged at Marwell Zoo, head-scratchingly entitled 'What A Lot You Can Do for the Ocelot'. Give me Glenda and her piano doing 'I Am the Walrus' any time.

21 My Boys. And Me

A Few of Our Favourite Things

On the whole, my two children get on about as well as – possibly better than – most siblings of their ages do. This opinion is clearly based on thorough and objective research into the subject of how well children with three and a half years between them get along with each other and has no basis whatsoever on favourable parental bias. This mutual tolerance – they even seem to like each other at times – is, I would like to think, due in no small part to sound and patient parental guidance. But they are people, not casts or imprints. They are good – better than average – kids because they choose to be so. Again, this is based on exhaustive comparative tests, which means I have seen enough of other people's children to know I am glad to have the two I do.

Despite the fact that they get on well, and are tremendously appreciative of the other's needs (i.e. they are aware that other people have needs), it is still sometimes a challenge to come up with activities that will entertain both of them without reducing their brains to a pulp of video games and television. Gabriel is going through a phase of not being able to see the point of doing anything unless it involves a football, and if it is not made of plastic and does not transform from a tank to a lion, or an elephant to a motorbike then Dylan simply does not want to know. The trouble is that Dylan (and I must try to be sensitive and fatherly about this) currently seems to have two left feet and has so far demonstrated nothing on the football pitch as much as huge potential for a future minister of silly walks, and Gabriel now denies all knowledge of ever having been entertained by the Power Rangers.

Although both boys usually make a creditable effort to show an interest in each other's games, it invariably becomes apparent that their hearts really aren't beating the same rhythm. Somehow, though, the allotment has recently captivated the boys to an extent that has surprised me. They perhaps see it as a chance to get out in the fresh air, have a bit of a giggle and indulge their boyish obsessions with dirty, slimy things. Another possibility is that it is simply my enthusiasm and optimism which has rubbed off on them. They see that it makes me happy and fulfilled and, perhaps because they have endured me in some of my deeper pits of futility and misery, anything that makes even a grumpy old sod like me a little sunnier must have something to it. As parents, we are so busy worrying about whether or not our children are happy that we often forget that they have similar concerns for us.

So it is perhaps a little ironic that this weekend, which I had intended to spend exclusively at the plot with indulgent picnics and easy gardening, the boys have both had parties to go to. Gabriel yesterday and Dylan today. Along with Gabriel's football training yesterday morning and our traditional Sunday-morning laziness, this left little scope for us doing one of the things we can enjoy collectively. I tried to see this as an opportunity, not a problem, as it would give me a decent length of time to spend with the boys individually, boring each of them as stiff as a board with lectures on potatoes, gardening, life cycles and all manner of things which mean nothing whatsoever to them.

Dylan did not really know what he wanted to plant yesterday afternoon, and he wasn't entirely sure what the options were. Asking a five-year-old what vegetable he would like to grow, based on what he would eventually like to eat, is a little like asking someone wearing dentures which flavour of toffee they would prefer. It is cruel and pointless. So, in order to induce a decision, it was necessary to enlist the assistance of all those senses not responsible for finding root crops entirely repugnant (i.e. all except taste).

Naturally he was happy to grow anything that looked like something Bugs Bunny would eat, and I think that his decision to grow peas was based wholly on the noise they made in the packet. Although not the reason for ordering specific varieties (they all sound the same to me), my desire to grow peas was at least in part due to these acoustic qualities – not to mention that curiously delicious feeling, when holding the packet flat on the hand and tipping it round and around, of those shrivelled orbs rolling over the palm through their prophylactic paper. I used to do this as a child, in the garden with my father, and I wonder if he had the same awareness of the import and durability of these experiences as I try to have with my boys now.

Speaking of which, I have learned an important lesson recently – that it takes roughly twice the amount of time to do anything on an allotment with kids around than it does to do it on your own. I am at pains to point out that this is no way due to incompetence on the boys' part, but is more down to their insistence on pretending that each gardening implement is a weapon of some kind before doing anything remotely agricultural with it. Once the appropriate tool is selected and redesignated, they will then proceed to stab, shoot, club or flog imaginary foes of the allotment holder (supermarket managers, city councillors, urban planners, spaniels, etc.). A trowel can easily be mistaken for a gun (especially by a tetchy and tired policeman), and Dylan's remarkably imaginative reinvention of a garden line as a pair of nunchakus really is something to behold.

Dylan and I stared at what has been designated his and Gabriel's bed. I explained that first we had to push the nunchaku handles in at either side, with the string stretched tight between them.

When I was in my first term at art college, studying for what has turned out to be an exceptionally relevant and worthwhile degree in silversmithing and jewellery, I was asked by one of my lecturers whether I had ever 'drawn down wire'. Bearing in mind that my only previous experience of metalwork had been in bending paper clips backwards and forwards until they broke because I liked the ash-white colour they went just before they did so, I think my confusion was understandable. I scoured my brain for reasons why I would want to draw down wire – a ruler, set square or French curve certainly, but wire? Surely it would bend all over the place. Who would hold the other end while I held the pencil, or did I have to use my teeth?

Before he told me that drawing down wire was in fact a process by which you reduce the sectional shape and/or size of a length of wire by pulling it through ever smaller holes, I looked at Nick that day with an expression similar to Dylan's when I told him that we now had to 'draw a drill'. I explained what this meant, putting to rest any concerns about not having any felt-pens or paper with us. He also seemed much happier at having his nunchakus in the soil now he knew why.

That scratch in the soil – made predominantly by Dylan – was the straightest so far on the plot; a feat of dexterity and control I found both rewarding and mildly surprising considering that often it is all he can do to remain on both feet and not crash into the furniture. Dylan is the sort of child who likes nothing better than a 'who can stand on one leg the longest' or a 'who can spin round and round the most without falling over' competition (usually against himself). When he gets really bored, he will try both at the same time, usually while singing or grinning at the pure joy of being alive. A truly exceptional little boy.

He also proved very adept at sowing the carrot seeds, tiny as they are. Maybe because his dimpled and genetically askew fingers could make more sense of their scale. As it was the weekend, and I was feeling a little cavalier by that point, I allowed him to get away with half an inch of compost over the top of them as opposed to 12.7 mm.

After this, we moved the string along a boot or so in order to get a row of peas in. I showed Dyl how to use the flat base of the hoe this time, as opposed to the corner we had just employed for the carrots. Peas need to be sown in a wide, flat-bottomed drill, and as we pulled the hoe towards us, my calloused palms overlapping his tender hands, I realized that the earth leaves its scars on our tools in the form of scratches and peeled paint, just as the tools themselves rub off on us, leaving blisters and hard skin. And, like steel, we become harder and more brittle where we have been hit the most often.

Dylan did as the seed packet recommended and scattered the shrivelled spheres at a depth of 'about two inches', or precisely 50.8 mm. The pale apple-green peas looked strangely startled and isolated against the rich, coffee-bean brown of the compost, and it almost felt like cruelty to bury them, until I told myself to stop being such a melodramatic old bore, and that there doesn't have to be portent and poetry in absolutely everything I do.

After we had funereally flung and firmed the oppressive, dark, cold clods of earth over the gasping, pleading and wailing orbs that were the peas, entombing them in both cradle and grave, Dylan said that all the work we had done had made him feel 'zorsted'. To emphasize this, he slumped and panted theatrically (the only way Dylan does pretty much anything) and lay down on the springy grass path next to where we had been working. As well as the planting, he had made a fine job of removing any final large stones and small weeds from the bed while I had turned over part of the one adjacent to it. We had had a lovely afternoon, and had both learned some pretty important stuff; Dylan, that peas should be sown four times deeper than carrots and that it is possible to draw a drill with a hoe. For my part, I realized that it is not only the fact that they can be sown which makes ideas similar to seeds – it is also that they won't see the light of day if they are planted too deeply.

Today, I made the executive decision (a thinly veiled euphemism for 'I'm still bigger and uglier than both of you put together so we're doing it anyway') to not lounge around in bed and instead go up to the plot in the morning. I didn't want to rely on the time that

Gabriel and I would have while Dylan was partying later, mainly because I wasn't sure whether that would give us enough time to do what we had planned before picking the Small One up. Both boys were amenable to this suggestion – helped, no doubt, by the large, well-lit dome of blue sky outside.

Gabriel was keen to do some digging, which was lucky as this was just what his part of their bed needed before anything was sown in it. Once again, and while Dylan was busy decapitating imaginary spaniels with a bamboo cane, I was at pains to impart the finer points of fork technique to Gabriel, particularly because I remembered the pain that he was in the day after the last time he knew how to do it. This time he seemed interested in what I had to say – perhaps because he too remembered that pain, but I suspect it was mainly because he knew damn well that if he tried to ignore me, I'd go all misty-eyed while talking about my Dad and 'letting the tool do the work'. He knew that if he listened, I would shut up quicker.

Whether or not my paternal wisdom made any difference I can't say, but whatever inspired him, he did a bloody good job – assiduously removing all the weeds and any of the rocks which 'looked as if they might cause trouble' – my deliberately ambiguous and, I hoped, empowering answer to Gabe's question of which ones he should take out. What this reply actually meant was 'You've got as much idea as I have, mate', but if I'd said that he might not have taken the digging talk so seriously.

As we drew the drill for the carrots, I admonished myself for assuming that I might have to give the bed a once-over after he had finished, in order to remove any bits that he had missed. There were none, and I reminded myself that as much as I should never take my children for granted, and should always be appreci-ative of the fact that they can walk, talk, run, play football, pretend to be dogs and are capable of a whole host of other activities that many children, tragically, are not, I must not be at all surprised when they dem-onstrate supreme competence. After all, they're *my* kids, which obviously means that they can do absol-utely anything, without needing anyone to tell them how to do it.

Dylan had now turned his attention to gunning down the local Tesco's manager with a hand-fork, while I gently helped to guide the draw hoe in Gabriel's hands – more out of the pleasure of togetherness than necess-ity. I think he also knew he could do it alone, but he too sensed that this was an opportunity to allow my 'Daddy' persona to feel wanted and useful. As it turned out, the drill was as straight as a dog's hind leg. This was either due to us both being distracted by the warm glow of paternal bonding, or because we were pulling in different directions – trying to feel our way through the earth according to contrasting preferences or sensibilities. It won't be the last time. He is growing up fast. Faster than me now.

As directed, he sprinkled the carrot seed thinly onto the compost which he had evenly crumbled and spread, and covered them with roughly half an inch of the same. Because he is that much older than Dylan, I admonished him for his sloppiness in this latter regard, and reminded him that I had quite clearly stated that the seeds were to be covered with 12.7 mm.

His plaintive response – so full of contrition and candour – will stay with me forever: 'Up yours, you boring old tosser – I'm gonna help Dyl sort out that stuffed suit.'

And there was me saying it was difficult to find things that they like doing together.

There was no time for manager mauling, though. Time had snuck up behind us, tapped us on the shoulder and said, 'BOO!' We had to pack up and get home in order to wipe various substances – mud, snot, tea-dunked choc-chip cookies, last night's tomato sauce, spaniel's blood – from Dylan's face before he went on the pull. Hanging the tools back in the shed reminded me that I must have a word with Steve about this very activity. When I had banged the nails in, I did so in a formation based on the pendulous needs of each individual tool, and the whole arrangement works very nicely if the tools are hung in the right sequence, the right way round. But every time Steve tidies up, it looks as if it's been done by someone from Devon.

On the way to Dylan's party, Gabriel said, in a voice which usually precedes an unfeasible request or major admission, 'Daddy?'

'Yes, mate.'

'Do you mind if we don't go to the plot this afternoon and do something else instead?'

I found myself wondering whether his trepidation was due to not wanting to disappoint me or not wanting to receive another tirade of paternal twaddle. Probably a combination of the two, but what was significant to me was the fact that Gabe has obviously developed the sensitivity to be at least in part aware of what the allotment has come to mean to me, and did not want to disappoint. I assured him that no, this would not be a problem and suggested a game of football at the park instead. His relief was palpable, no doubt because he wouldn't have to spend the afternoon ankle deep in mud, listening to his old man going on about How Lucky We Are. Nine-year-old boys do not need philosophical discussion anywhere near as much as they need help with curling a football or the offside rule.

Every half-decent parent will understand that there are no words which can adequately express how, nor indeed how much, we love our children, and will also appreciate why I find it astonishing that other parents can profess to loving their offspring as much as I do mine. But I have recently realized – or have stopped denying – that I am also quite self-absorbed, and can get somewhat restless if I don't get to close down in my own space and within my own mind once in a while. I find it very hard to be close to someone unless there is some distance between us. Time which we can genuinely call our own is a rare vegetable, and I like to appreciate it and value it not in *preference* to being with the boys, but as a chance to do all sorts of stuff which, were I to write it down, would sound awfully Californian.

So this evening, after I had dropped the boys at their mother's house, I pottered back to the plot, leaving both the car and Charlie at home on the way. The last thing I needed was him going on about letting the stick do the work in his silly, doggy way. Actually, that was the second-to-last thing I needed. The final straw would be getting nicked while driving back from the plot after the four-pack I was going to sink while I was there. After being responsible for the kids for five days, I wanted to let my hair down and go wild. For me, now, that means a quartet of Stellas while I am, if only nominally, watering my peas. That – not counting Glenda – is about as Rock and Roll as it gets.

As I wandered back and forth with the watering can, in a haze of one-part peaceful contemplation and one-part cold beer on a warm evening, my mind drifted to the kind of thoughts only possible when surrounded by silence and beauty. The clocks sprang forwards last night, and the extra daylight was as welcome and warm as a returning lover. I realized that I had never found a satisfactory answer to the question as to why this chronological anomaly actually occurs. This confusion has never been helped by the expression 'Daylight Saving Time', as it is patently nonsense. As far as I can see, we don't actually save any daylight at all – we just move it about a bit in order to make winter seem all the more appalling. It must simply be some curiously 'British' thing – that maybe we still haven't quite got over the loss of the empire, and if we can't tell the weather (what *would* we talk about?) or Johnny Foreigner what to do, then we'll bally well push time around instead.

I don't want to complain about it today, though, because as it was I got an extra hour in which to get the beds suitably damp and myself more firmly planted. After I had lugged as many watering cans as it took to give them all a good soaking, I sat on the step up to the shed. The blue-grey and downy peach of the sunset seemed to welcome me back, and everyone else had seen fit to stay away. As I sat, isolated and listening to myself breathe, I cast my eye over the plot, and my mind six months backwards to a time when we had been faced with metre-high grasses and gnarled obsolescences. Unfortunately, I was only just starting to take photographs – and photography – seriously then, so don't have an awful lot of visual evidence of what it was like (I think Lizzie has a couple of shots), but in my mind's eye it was infinitely easier to visualize how the plot looked last September than it was to imagine the ordered, ranked and weeded rows of vegetables we desired, often chosen as much for their sonorous qualities as for their epicurean ones. In the six months since we had started, we had actually come further along than we ever thought we would. Stevie and I agreed recently that if, when we first attacked the plot, we had been offered then what we have there now, we would have laughed first, then accepted it without reserve. Similarly, if someone had suggested that my 'allotment diary perhaps' would have grown to fill a lever arch file, I would have been equally sceptical. But the words are there – not necessarily in the right order – and if those beds don't grow anything after all we've done, then the whole lot – pages and pea sticks – might as well end up on the fire.

As I left the plot, I appreciated the fact that I was able to do so by using the system of paths created by the positive and regular shapes of the beds, as opposed to having to hack my way through as I would have done half a year ago. I hazily and optimistically checked the beds for signs of swelling seeds and thrusting shoots, but neither lager nor euphoria are strong enough to be hallucinogenic, and all I saw was bed 'b', staked down at either side like a taut groundsheet and uninterrupted save for 137 onion tips, as it had been earlier. But because we had managed to get to this stage without getting either bored or disillusioned, the possibility of snapping our own peas and unearthing our own Foremosts seemed within our grasp, and under our control.

22 Pleasure and Rain

Morning Bloody Glory

1 April

For a number of reasons, today and yesterday have been
two of the most contrary consecutive days I think I've
ever experienced. I've been trying to work out which of
those reasons made the most marked difference to the
distinct flavours of each. Inevitably, on this isle, it is the
Weather.

Of course the Great British Obsession with the

Weather is now cliché, which by definition also makes it the whole truth. It is something which, no matter how diverse the colours, careers, social status, wealth, intelligence or beliefs of this nation, we can all unite in either enjoying or bemoaning. It is one of a precious few common grounds with sufficient acreage for all members of a society which has been an amalgam of different cultures for as long as this lump of rock has been inhabited. The symbols for the weather forecast on television weren't cooked up in some graphic design studio – they were traced from the walls of a Neanderthal cave in North Wales.

Not everyone has suffered haemorrhoids or in-growing toenails but surely everybody has at some point experienced the discomfort, ignominy and inconvenience of flapping about like a wet flannel after being told by some irritatingly perky weather forecaster, with a smile as bright and wide as the sun itself that we could leave the brollies at home. 'Predictable weather' – in this country – is a contradiction in everybody's terms.

We talk about the weather a lot, then, because it is kind of interesting in its capriciousness. We also talk about it because it often plays a fundamental role in some of our greatest – not to mention oddest – national pastimes. For the sporting enthusiast, there is cricket and tennis and it is in these, for us Brits, truly the taking part that counts. I suspect that we may be able to participate much more effectively if we didn't have to keep running on and off the pitch/court when it randomly, heavily and unpredictably pisses down.

There are some sports, of course, which are not so dependent on the weather, and indeed are actually much more fun to watch when the rain and wind are howling around the protagonists, especially when you are watching in a pub with a log fire. There is more to this than schadenfreude, however. There is something undeniably stirring about watching 450 stone of men chasing a slippery, funny-shaped ball around a large, muddy rectangle, as much as there is something amusing about watching twenty-two overpaid, overrated and over-inflated boys slicing a wet football. The fun to be had from watching golfers getting wet through to the inside in the squally rain is, though, entirely different – this is very definitely due to schadenfreude. But to be bound to an outdoor sport in this country, especially one in which we have no choice but to cheer for the plucky underdog is, to a lesser or greater extent, also to be tied to the weather.

We are also obsessed with the weather because, as a tiny island, we are bombarded with it from all sides and directions. Dotted around the coastline are thousands of families whose livelihoods depend in no small part on the vagaries of the weather, and of course gardening, on a domestic or commercial scale, is also hugely reliant on the comings and goings of our climate. It follows that the seasons dictate what happens when, and certain activities are only possible and/or advisable at predetermined, or allotted, times.

We have a national fascination with the weather which extends as far as being able to talk to complete strangers about it without – and indeed often to cover up – any embarrassment. Unless you have no interest in appropriate dress, sport, fishing, farming or gardening, you will be glued to the weather forecast along with everyone else.

And it is precisely this changeability which has made the last two days so remarkable – true, they also had entirely different agendas, and yesterday was March and today is April, but it's as if the thirty-first and the first did some kind of meteorological, structural and chronological 'do-si-do', and switched not only partners but also clicked their heels back to winter again.

Yesterday, I spent the entire day at the plot, carrying on from where I had beerily moseyed off on Sunday evening. A highly productive day, during which I planted stuff, moved things around, whistled tunelessly to myself, threw sticks for the dog, drank tea and wrote in my journal. At 11.35 a.m., I had this to say:

This is what it's all about. Although having said that, I can't help questioning what 'it all' is. Try this. Charlie is lying at my feet and in the sun, having had a tough morning lying in the sun in lots of other places. The only sounds I can hear are birdsong (including the belligerent but still melodious cawing of a distant pheasant), the scritch-clang of a rake being pulled back and forth over the dry earth and tumbling stones by somebody three plots south-west of me and the irregular, angular flapping of a triangle of perished blue polythene being lifted by the slight breeze and tapped against the side of a shed (to which it is loosely stapled) to my left. Once again, it is warm enough to make a T-shirt one item of clothing too many when digging, and I'm mopping the triangle of sweat which gathers in the middle of my chest by pressing my top against it. Sweating is like getting dirty or bloody – it denotes that you have been doing something purposeful. However, it doesn't feel as if I've come here for show today, although getting sweaty, dirty and bloody are three of digging's great bonuses. It truly feels as if I came here to dig, amongst doing other things, purely for the enjoyment of doing so. The hard work and backache involved are also part of that enjoyment – in fact they are a crucial element of it.

An hour or so later, I added this:

Grub squashing is another pleasant pastime which occasionally breaks the monotony of hitting clods of soil with your fork (or fist if you are not bloody enough). I have read an illuminating and erudite section in one of my books, entitled 'Creepy Crawlies – Nice or

ALLOTTED TIME

Nasty?'. Worms are good – everyone knows that, and I still have
enormous trouble believing the consolation that, if I slice one in half,
then the two segments will grow into two distinct worms. Does that
mean they've both got a head and a bum? It seems as likely to me
as being able to put little baby onions in the soil and pull big, soupy
onions out a few months later. Other grubs include millipedes (bad),
all tight and spiralled like miniature and very neat cumberland
sausages, and centipedes (good) which always seem to be in a hurry
and as if they could use an extra pair of hands. There are also the
fat, creamy-coloured ones with leathery brown heads which I have
been squashing with just a little more pleasure than I should probably
be admitting to. This vendetta is based not on any hard facts as to
whether they are 'nice' or 'nasty', but on the opinion that anything
that looks as if it would have really given me the willies had it been
magnified 1,000 times and appeared on <u>Dr Who</u> is probably not
going to be any good for the plot either. I have tried to find out
what these things are so that I can kill them with more
justification (and without the creeping fear that I may be
destroying creatures which are actually really nice to carrots), but I
am afraid that one ugly grub looks much like another, so splat it is.
This may offend the sensibilities of some, but the front line of
organic control over anything obnoxious is the bottom of your boot.
Speaking of which, I've read quite a bit of stuff about slug control
(eggshells, scissors, coffee, beer, night raids, etc.) recently but not one
tome has mentioned the most effective method of permanently
eliminating these molluscs. It involves no violence, chemicals, tools or

other extraneous substances. It is also dazzlingly simple. Steve and I came up with it one night a few weeks ago, and it is this: do not grow anything that slugs like to eat.

And just after lunch, this happened:

Ron and Joyce ambled past a few minutes ago. After I had assured them that their sprouts had gone down extremely well (not down my throat, but still appreciated by my folks), thank you, we chatted about what we had 'got in'. I pointed at our rows of bamboo sticks and mumbled apologetically about the seeds we had naively sown between them and about how we were hoping for some beginners' luck. Ron folded his arms and shook his head. While fixing me with a knowing eye and an avuncular smile he said, 'There's no such thing.'

He seemed really quite sure in the way that people who know what they are talking about are when what they are talking about is not really what they are talking about at all. Ron didn't expand on this statement before he departed, but left his words dangling and shimmering in the air, ready to be tarnished by interpretation.

I think he meant that novices try harder. They try harder because they are nearer to, and therefore a great deal more aware of, the likelihood of failure. With experience inevitably comes a greater degree of complacency or insouciance – mind and muscle memory take over. The experience is also diminished as it becomes practised – this, I think, is why I rarely finish anything. When we learn a new process, we are always told to get to grips with the basics first; in the same way that the trunk of a tree informs the rest of its shape, these fundamentals tell us how any particular system of knowledge works and what its branches look like. Common sense tells me that it is unwise to forget these underpinnings in favour of the blind search for greater complexity and sophistication.

It is hard to overestimate or overstate just how dazzling yesterday was. There was, quite simply, nothing wrong with it, and I'm not sure I'd have all my fingers down if I counted off how many days I have had in my life on the skin of which I could not find a single blemish. Everything happened when I wanted it to, the sun slowly, gently and evenly roasted me all day, Charlie did what dogs do at the park on a hot day without offending anyone. Ken showed up, but for some reason was quieter and capable of hearing, so we had such a pleasant chat that I can't even recall what it was about, and not only did I sit and write quite a bit, I was also very productive on the plot. I finished digging over what was left of the boys' bed (only two or three rows), finished weeding and turning over bed 'f', started to do the same to bed 'd' at the bottom of the plot, put in a row of peas for Gabriel, leaving space for the garlic I'm going to put there tomorrow, and planted all thirty-eight of our First Early (Foremost) potatoes in two rows of thirteen, one of twelve. I stretched a warm, green, taut line down bed 'a' and dug holes to the depth of my trowel handle at intervals of eighteen inches (somehow it seems okay to plant potatoes in imperial), measured with a cut cane. Into every hole I placed a handful each of compost and damp newspaper as recommended by Hugh Fearnley-Whittingstall's dad in Hugh's *River Cottage Cookbook*. On top of this I placed a tuber, the shoots like purple-blue tentacles grasping skyward. Occasionally, however wrong it felt to do so, I cut the larger ones in half. Apparently, providing each piece has at least two chits protruding from it, it will be fine. Maybe it does work with worms. I then moved the line a couple of boots or so for each row. When they were all interred, I 'earthed them up' by forming a straight apex of soil over them with the draw hoe. A process we will need to repeat as they grow in order to ward off blight and increase yield. I found the whole process to be so enjoyable that finishing turned out to be something of a disappointment, and compared with the effort to likely viability ratio of the carrots, the spuds seem like racing certainties.

I also came home and attended to the tomato plants which, although growing well enough, still have kinked stems from when I had turned them round. As with all things kinky, today I tied them up good and proper, in this case to their individual bamboo canes. They now

look much more businesslike, not to mention an average
of four inches taller and, although tomatoes aren't
exactly my idea of culinary nirvana, the plants do make
the bedroom smell fantastic, especially on a bright
spring morning when they have been watered the night
before.

No danger of that, though, this morning. Not only did
they not get watered last night, but the weather seemed
to have forgotten where it was today. I assumed at first
that I must have woken up earlier than usual, but as I
flopped over to resume sleeping I caught sight of the
bedroom clock. It was half past eight, and it was still
dark. I was concerned, as I came to, that the last four
months had not, in fact, happened at all, that we had
been plunged back into the grim abyss of winter, and
that I should have gone round to Sue's last night to pick
up the seeds. I tried to decide what would be worse
about this scenario – that we hadn't actually done any
of the work described here and had to do it all again,
or that I had had a dream about six months on an
allotment. The rest of the day, weather-wise, was wall-
to-wall gloom and greyness. It was also as unseason-
ably cold as yesterday was incongruously warm, and I
glanced at my shorts forlornly as I dressed myself for

what was to be a day of chasing two rabbits and catching neither and fishing for red-herrings. Perhaps it was just yesterday that had been a dream.

But I checked the plot on my way home, and all that I thought I'd got done yesterday was still expectantly lined and earthed up. There is now more stuff in the ground which is supposed to be there, and slightly less which isn't, which means that everything must be okay, and, despite today's frustrations and dampness, yesterday still stands as a warm, glowing reminder of how 'it all' sometimes can be.

4 April

Plan for the day: walk the dog and buy milk from the local shop. Get out into the 'garden' and weed around the garlic and raspberries as well as blast as many other weeds as possible. Make beds for and sow the leeks. Water them in. Lunch. Up to the plot with watering can, plant labels, pencil, journal, flask. Plant some peas and another row of carrots. Water and label all rows. Throw chicken-shit pellets over garlic. Dig some stuff into bed 'd' before planting peas (just remembered!). Back home. Greenhouse.

The above was what I set down in my journal earlier as some kind of yardstick against which I could measure today's progress in my developing relationship with the allotment. Like all successful relationships, gardening takes a bit of hard work but hey, you don't get the pleasure if there ain't no pain.

Pain. In the bleeding arse. I am referring to bindweed. This morning, I wanted to fuel my growing obsession with the stuff by levering some more of it up with a hand-fork. It truly is quite remarkable. Today, amongst scores of others, I dug up one piece whose tip was only about an inch above the surface – a milky-white stem unfurling a telltale heart-shaped dark green leaf. I dug to well over the length of the hand-fork (including handle) before I could feel that it would come out without snapping. Its root consisted of a half-inch length of shrivelled and maggot-like piece of string. An eloquent and forceful reminder of the blinkered, selfish, and seemingly unstoppable struggle for the perpetuation of life. The bindweed has started to come up and out with some force now, and there is only so much I can dig out without snapping the roots, so I have decided to take drastic action in the form of a spray bottle of Tumbleweed. Not, I realize, the most organically sound of garden products, but it was either this or me continuing to very effectively propagate the species by chopping its roots into lots of tiny pieces, or 'digging them up', as I have been optimistically calling it.

Apparently, Tumbleweed is a 'systemic' weedkiller, which means that it kills stuff from the inside out, being absorbed by the leaves and taken down to the roots. It is also 'non-residual' and 'biodegradable' which sounds kind of responsible and friendly in an I-know-I'm-having-the-wool-pulled-over-my-eyes-but-it-suits-me-right-now kind of way. I wandered about the 'garden', zapping as much of the bindweed as I could without getting too near the raspberries and their interplanted companions the garlic cloves, both of which seem to be doing fine. I hand-weeded around them, as I was going to water them later and saw no point in doing the same favour for the ever-lurking bindweed and the brace of alarmingly large thistles which must have landed and thrust their gratuitously ugly taproots into the soil over-night.

The fact that most operations – garden-related or otherwise – seem to take approximately two and a quarter times as long as their original estimate is one that has amazed and irked me for some time. Even if this is taken into account at the start, most tasks seem still to drag on for far longer than planned. I realized today that it is generally not the jobs themselves which take inordinate amounts of time to complete; rather it is all the smaller, peripheral activities, which prove necessary in order to facilitate the Main Event, that eat

time like black holes swallow light. Weeding the raspberries and garlic, for example, takes hardly any time at
all, but finding the gardening gloves (well they *were* BIG
thistles) takes just over twice as long again, as I discovered this morning.

After I had done the various bits of weeding and
spraying (including finding the Tumbleweed, figuring
out which way to point it and fully comprehending the
instructions) I foolishly turned to the altogether more
complex task of preparing two raised beds in which we
could sow our leek seeds. On the face of it, the procedure looked reasonably straightforward:

1 Take two sections of vertically stacking compost bin
   donated by Mother.
2 Line bottoms of above with rubble to provide drainage.
3 Sift soil from proposed 'lawn' area of 'garden' and mix
   with compost from bag.
4 Flatten ready for sowing.

Easy, right? A doddle! Until you realize that to effect 1,
first you must move twenty or so pieces of brittle, jagged
and almost humanly unpredictable sheets of glass once
destined – before their sudden and bizarre breakages –
for the greenhouse, as they are currently leaning against
the required wooden structures. After eyeing up this
glass in the same way you would rotten fruit on a

market stall, your attention turns to 2, and you remember that most of the 'rubble' went to the tip a couple of months ago, so you will have to 'make' some by hitting a couple of spare paving slabs quite hard with a lump hammer. This makes you feel slightly better because the sole justification for their still being in the 'garden' – 'that they might come in handy one day' is now vindicated. Then your mood is dragged back to where it was by remembering that they only missed the trip to the tip in the first place because they were still in one piece.

'Sifting soil', naturally, is a euphemism for 'finding soil' when it comes to the 'lawn' area, covered as it is with anything which is growing at this time of year. In addition to this, this area of wasteland is also home to dozens of very unpleasant and irregular curves of splintered glass – the reasons for the shapes of the pieces of glass leaning in the way of point 1. In order to remove these, some kind of receptacle was required, and all I could think of was a bin bag, which I thought would surely split once any argument between the glass and gravity flared up.

At least theoretically, 4 was easy enough, but did depend entirely on the previous three points being carried out successfully, which immediately led me to wonder whether there was any realistic chance it would get done before nightfall.

ALLOTTED TIME

In actuality, although there was indeed a dark echo of dusk in the 'garden' by the time I'd finished, the setting up of the leek beds was rather enjoyable (apart from the bits involving glass, of course – the smaller pieces of which I found a box for, the larger pieces I made into smaller pieces and found another box for). Flat soil may not grow plants any better than humpy stuff, but in this case somehow it seemed comforting to add a third dimension of perpendicularity to the two already formed by the squareness of the box it is in. We seem conditioned, in the 'developed' world, to try to dominate nature by making it square, flat, orderly, named, formal and geometric – it is ironic that our box-like domestic and automotive creations and our compartmentalization of nature often serve only, ultimately, to make us increasingly alienated from it. Perhaps it is true that the more control we feel we are losing to anonymous people in grey suits and in grey call centres, the more we desire to compensate by the domination of that which remains subordinate to us. But the earth isn't like those grey-suited people – the soil listens to you. What's more, it will never make you listen to Beethoven's Ninth played on a Stylophone while it puts you on hold.

I didn't sow the leek seeds today. Instead, they are in their opened inner packets in front of me as I write. I took a peek at them earlier – each no larger than a comma written with a free-flowing pen. As I paused a minute or so ago, silent, still and chasing an elusive word, I was sure I could hear them murmuring expectantly – as if they knew I had made their bed, and wanted to go and lie on it. A strange awakening – soon to be an eruption. I find myself wanting to watch – to convince myself that I can see them grow in the same way that, at primary school, I liked to make myself believe that if I sat still for long enough, I would be able to see the hour hand move on the classroom clock. Some people never even stop for long enough to appreciate just one second.

5 April

Today at the plot, despite my continuing misgivings concerning underestimated timescales, and once I'd got over the shock of having remembered to bring everything I needed, I managed to surprise myself by carrying out most of what I'd planned to do up there. The sowing may not have been done with quite the solemnity and reverence as it was the first time, but was achieved competently and efficiently and anyway, stuff grows, right? Mum told me. Bed 'd' didn't end up getting any attention whatsoever, but I had already decided against putting any peas in there at that point for reasons which now elude me. It could have been to do with the wind direction.

I also saw Ted for the first time in over a fortnight. I think his week-long holiday had started just as I was returning from Cornwall. He seemed to be in fine spirits, and relayed some of the high points of his and his wife's European coach tour. His buffed Hampshire brogue momentarily fooled me into thinking that he'd said '*Couch* Tour', which brought to mind lovely images of Ted and Jean testing the relative merits of French and German sofas. Ted's most memorable experience, he said, was the guided tour of the Monaco Grand Prix track. For an instant, my imagination took me to a lovely place where Ted's coach party was locked head to head with another, and the fifty or so occupants of each ran from one side to the other while rounding the corners in an entertaining yacht/motor-racing hybrid before I remembered that the Monaco GP track is, for most of the year, a road, so the likelihood of anyone breaking any speed limits was slim. I mentioned the idea to Ted, though, and he seemed both excited by it as well as vaguely disappointed that it hadn't actually happened. But I think that Saga Coach Racing would be an event in the sporting calendar worth watching. You read it here first.

Before I went home, I managed to remember to pick up the watering can so I could water the leeks in; what I'd forgotten was that I hadn't actually sown them yet. However, the raspberries and garlic also needed refreshment, and by the time I had watered them, I knew that the leeks would have to wait yet longer.

I'd enlisted Steve's help last night after filling him in on the day's events. It seemed only fair to include him, as there are two beds and two varieties of leeks, therefore it seemed reasonable that Steve should do both while I sat around and tormented his dog.

'Sounds good, mate. Whatever.'

We drew lines as straight as our wobbly fingers would allow us, commenting on how we seemed to be creating a vegetable plot in miniature, and being reminded of how much we really feel as if we are playing God at the allotment. Which, as it happens, is not that philosophically straightforward when you are a born-again atheist. Metaphysical worries aside, it is tricky to think of anything interesting to relate about the sowing of leek seeds which I haven't banged on about before – we chucked them in, covered them up and shook earthy hands while heartily congratulating each other on another couple of quid and another half an hour wasted.

We then turned our delicate touch to the greenhouse in order to get it to a stage where it will be warmer on the inside than the ambient temperature outside. I have recently discovered that this is a prerequisite of similar importance to the upward orientation of the pointy bits, and I can't help thinking that we would have been much more circumspect about taking it on had this complication been made clear to us at the outset. However, false pretences or not, it was here now, so we felt we ought to do what we could. Which, if I am honest, I don't think is going to be quite enough. We have used up all of the sheets of glass which were either the right size or deigned to be cut to it, and we're now left with all the pieces that are from the wrong greenhouse and are therefore now in the wrong book. So, we resorted to the plastic sheeting 'donated' by a local and untidy carpet fitter, and a roll of masking tape. Apart from the odd infuriating incident involving strips of tape looping and irreversibly sticking to themselves in self-forming Mobius strips, and the ruffling of the polythene in the just-strong-enough-to-annoy breeze, we got on quite well, and the greenhouse looked much more sure of itself by the time we had finished. Were I to describe it now, using only one word, it would have to be 'plucky'. It has a few bits missing (indeed its east end is still virtually glassless), the glass that *is* present is of varying shapes, thicknesses and transparencies, and the door still needs a few judicious and precise nudges and taps before it will open. When we'd finished, we entered our new Thing Which We Had Built and felt noticeably warmer, but this was almost certainly due more to a combination of having just worked up a mild sweat and the inner glow of walking into something which we had constructed, than to the success of our 'glazing'.

Whichever it was, we had neither the materials nor the motivation to do any more so, as prematurely and optimistically as we had judged the shed complete (although now glazed it still has no felt on its roof), we deemed the greenhouse finished and ready to bring the Ailsa Craigs to ripeness and soft, red effulgence.

23 Floppy with a Yellow Bottom

They Look All Right to Me

20 April

I bloody hate gardening. It is a useless and pointless waste of time, energy and money. I can feel myself reverting to my long-held belief that the best garden is the one which is covered with four inches of concrete north to south, east to west, and that allotments are indeed only really suitable for those folk over eighty who can't get round Tesco's unaided.

Sunday effing morning, and I had had only five hours' sleep because I'd very sensibly elected to stay up until two this morning drinking and thinking with Simon, a friend from London, and because I was woken at seven o'clock by Charlie looking at me in a bemused fashion because Simon was lying on *his* sofa cushions and was attempting to hack up the contents of half of last night's cigarettes. I could also hear one or both of the boys mumbling and stirring. My eyes felt as if someone had swapped them over during the night using a pair of rusty pliers, and had inserted a mercury tilt-switch, plugged directly into the mains, inside my head. Every time I tried to move, I felt vaguely nauseous and had to close my eyes tightly.

Gabriel came in first, as he often does. On any other day, his slipping into bed all warm, soft and smelly for a sleepy morning snooze is a real treat and the best possible start to the day. Today, though, it meant that I was faced with a nine-year-old who had clearly done all the sleeping he was going to do for one night, thank you, and now wanted to look at cameras in the catalogues with me. Normally a joy, but how could I tell this little man that Daddy couldn't possibly get up until he could remember his own name, and that if Daddy had to sit up and focus on something then he would probably either vomit or cry or both?

'Juzgimmearvanourrwillyamate?'

Remarkably, and patently, he understood, because he did indeed go back to bed, poring over the Jessops catalogue, and came back what certainly felt like thirty minutes later, minus the catalogue. He slipped under the duvet, put his right arm across my stomach and rested his head on my shoulder. I turned my head away so as not to inflict my stale-beer breath on him; it might knock him out. I turned it back again. Anything for peace.

'Yeaghh! Your breath smells, Daddy.'

Not badly enough, obviously. Gabe wriggled up and, in an attempt to replace this stench, opened the curtains to check on the tomatoes.

'Your tomatoes have died, Daddy.'

'Huh!'

'They all look a bit, well, floppy.'

Fantastic. Bloody brilliant. I had spent the last five hung-over minutes fretting about the state of the green-house and its flailing, stupid bits of masking tape now detached from the polythene and most of the frame (leave masking tape on a window pane for a couple of days and it'll never budge, but polythene obviously isn't good enough for it). 'Jesus,' I thought, 'I bloody hate gardening. I have no greenhouse worth growing any-thing in or writing about, a dump for a garden and now

I've got dead bastarding tomatoes as well.' I was sure that there must have been something else. That was it – cats. And spaniels. And nearly all my onions died. I searched for a Point to It All, and drew a blank. As I lay in bed, I came to realize that I was not going to be able to sleep again for at least another fourteen hours, so resigned myself to getting up. And to going where? I didn't want to disturb Simon, who sounded as if he had settled down again after his earlier spluttering; getting into Gabriel's bed would have disturbed Dylan, which would only have complicated matters further. And I didn't want to stay where I was because all I could think of there was dead Ailsa Craigs. The kitchen, despite its obvious advantages of a kettle and breakfast equipment, wasn't too appealing either due to its absence of any-where to sit except its cold plastic floor. I felt like a piece in one of those puzzles whose aim is to make a picture out of eight interlocking but movable squares in a three-by-three grid – except I was the square that gets wedged, askew and stuck between its seven neighbours and the one blank space. That blank space was the bathroom. I un-wedged myself from bed, and went to sit down.

After as long as it had taken for my legs to go numb, I came up with a plan – Simon could have Gabriel's bed as Dylan had come to by then, while I went and rebuilt the sofa, in which I could bury myself with the kids and a mug of tea and watch some news to stop me from thinking how stupid and shit gardening is, how equally awful this book is and, consequently, how bloody lousy all of my life is. But Simon too had admitted the inevitability of wakefulness, so we drank a brew and had one of those extraordinarily difficult conversations only possible with someone who you know and love well, but who, like you, only finds his real voice after dark. Luckily, we didn't have to try too hard, as the boys were clamouring to start their Easter egg hunt. I blessed myself for having hidden the eggs last night, then immediately cursed as I couldn't remember where I'd put half of them. I did recall hiding an odd number of eggs, though; I just love watching them squabble. For the ones I couldn't remember, I made up some clues for likely sounding places and waited until they found something. Clues ranged from the cryptic – 'Some are green, some are blue, some are black but they are all re(a)d', to the simple – 'If I tell you it's in the big bowl in the kitchen, will that do for breakfast?'

The delight and excitement of these two pyjama'd angels lifted my spirits a little, but I still couldn't help thinking of the poor, wilting tomatoes, what the hell I was going to do about them and, perhaps more crucially, if they died, how would I then mask the smell in the bedroom?

On Thursday the boys and I had gone hunting for pea sticks. I was armed with three pieces of relevant information:

1 Peas grow to around 2 feet in height.
2 We needed sticks described on the packet as 'twiggy'.
  'Twiggy sticks' sounded like a tautology to me along similar lines to 'sticky logs'.
3 Climbing plants, apparently, do not like climbing up ash.

This last point could be sandal-wearing, tree-hugging piffle for all I know. In any event, I couldn't tell an ash stick from a breadstick right now, so I wasn't going to concern myself overmuch with this. Therefore we spent a very pleasant hour or so searching for twiggy sticks about 3 feet long. I was astonished at how many we managed to collect. I have lost count (in fact I never started) of how many times I have looked for a stick to throw for Charlie while walking round that park and not been able to find anything better than a sticky twig, yet there we were, overloading the barrow with so many good-sized sticks that it seemed as if they had literally started to grow on trees.

This afternoon, I left my hangover in Simon's eminently capable hands and took the boys up to the plot in order to push the sticks into the soil next to the very healthy-looking peas. Indeed, it was this very ebullience of the peas that prompted me into getting the sticks – if we'd left it much longer, they would have started to topple, unable to support their own success. By the time we had got up there, the boys' enthusiasm had met a similar fate, and they asked if I would mind if they took themselves off to the wilds of the park instead.

'No problem, just don't go any further than the swings.'

I'm not sure what it was that made them stop at the top of the plot, turn back and watch me neatly arranging a row of sticks; the possibility of building something useful, perhaps, or maybe it was the perceived chance to make a sculpture. But whether it was function or form, substance or style, they forewent striking out on their own in favour of doing some gardening with their daddy, and I am going to appreciate that for as long as it lasts. As long as they aren't still doing it when they are thirty.

Dylan arranged his sticks in the way that only Dylan could or would – remarkably neat in terms of their spacing and regularity at the bottom, but all jutting out in different directions, resulting in a manic scribble of twigs at the top. Gabriel, in turn, produced two lines of sticks which would have made Andy Goldsworthy shed a tear. The boys have good eyes. They worked so beautifully together today and, when I think about it, I don't remember them ever having had a cross word on the plot. Maybe at times in the park, when someone fouled someone else or one of them wanted to go home and the other didn't, but not on the allotment. Perhaps they really do sense that they are part of a larger whole, and therefore an awful lot closer to each other than they thought. Maybe I don't hate gardening.

As we approached the flat, I glanced up at my bedroom window, and saw the tomato plants – green, erect and soaking up the last of the dipping sun. I pointed them out to Gabriel.

'They look all right to me.'

'I guess – it was just that they looked a bit floppy and the bottom leaves had gone a bit yellow.'

I made something up about them being the first pair of leaves and how after a while the plant doesn't need them any more so they die. I had no idea what I was taking about, and am none the wiser now but the boys bought it, and even I started to think it was plausible by the time I had finished. I told them that they had probably gone 'floppy' this morning because I had been breathing on them for five hours. Gabriel could certainly relate to that.

But the tomatoes, despite being 'a bit floppy with yellow bottom leaves', are about to flower and, with a dab of decent tape on the greenhouse, should be fruiting by midsummer. I might even eat one. I don't hate gardening.

26 April

I didn't go to the plot immediately when we got home from my mother's place in Staffordshire yesterday, because it was eleven o'clock at night, and I wouldn't have been able to differentiate between our plot and Ted's, let alone check up on the onions. Instead, the boys and I ambled up there late this morning – possibly early this afternoon – armed with fig rolls, chocolate chip cookies, apples, skateboards, footballs and a dog. I really wanted to inspect the plot before any games commenced. Considering we had recently left it for just one night and some bloody dog had run over our beds, anything could have happened over the last four days – wildebeest, locusts, Ken's stick even. All was as it should have been, though. The peas were coming on well, some of their tendrils clingily grasping the sticks. There are now quite easily discernible rows of dark green and bushy carrot-tops. The onion sets are slicing the air with thick, sharp green fingers atop and compacting the earth by swelling silently below. The garlic stems are green and straight and thin and mean, hopefully in contrast to their multiplying and bulging bulbs. Even some of the onions which I have brought all the way from seed seem to be putting up a spirited fight, and one in particular has overtaken most, if not all, of the sets. I was slightly disappointed not to see any shoots in the swede bed, until I remembered that we had not sown any yet, but was overjoyed to see the mauve-tinged green of our first early potatoes blinking at me in the pale sun. I wanted to share with the boys my excitement at the fact that there was actually food growing on the allotment, but they had already made their way up to the park with the dog, the ball and, most significantly, the biscuits. I knew, though, that as I will hopefully see many potatoes grow during my life, I should really be taking advantage of every opportunity I have of seeing the boys do the same thing. Having them tell me how clever I am for burying three dozen potatoes could wait.

I took the boys back to their mother this afternoon and then went straight to the allotment with Steve to sit in the shed and sort the world out. Our plan, which we knocked up on the way, was to do some weeding, but the thin film of rain which we had walked through to get to the plot had thickened to sheets by the time we got there. We decided that it was too wet for any and all activities involving soil, so the weeds were temporarily reprieved.

I've noticed recently that I always feel out of rhythm when I have been away. At the risk of sounding ungrateful, however much it is possible to *feel* 'at home' in someone else's house, it is not until recently I have realized that this is not the same as *being* 'at home'. It's been some time since anywhere has felt like home to me and, consequently, that I've had any kind of rhythm to get out of. But in other people's homes you don't know which floorboards squeak in the same way you do your own and the door handles are all different and much too noisy late at night, when the slightest of movements become amplified. I love and depend on my mother, my sister and my brother-in-law utterly and unconditionally, but I am buggered if I can get into the stash of Choco Leibniz biscuits at 3.30 in the morning at either of their places without waking the entire house. But this 'coming home' is similar to putting on a dry wetsuit – you know it's yours, yet still it feels too small; as if it is constricting you. A little like wearing someone else's skin, until you start to flex and stretch yourself, when it begins to mould itself to you. Sitting in the shed with Steve, a flask and a spare hour or two, is one of the best ways that I have of getting to feel like my hide is my own again, and of feeling as if I have, finally, come home.

24 Making Our Own Beds

Weeded and Watered

30 April

Bugger.

I think I've killed the tomatoes.

Bugger. Arse and – what the hell – shit.

When I say 'I think', I really, deep down, mean to say 'I know'. However, there is mitigation and learning to be had, so all is not entirely lost – even if the plants are not going to bear any fruit, then at least I might benefit from some cuttings of wisdom.

Last week, I took three of these vibrant, vital and bushy (if a little floppy and yellow around the bottom) plants up for my mother as an alternative to cut flowers, chocolates or spending any money. I also wanted to prove that her good-for-nothing layabout of a son was doing something constructive with his time. She was delighted, but declared the plants in desperate need of 'pinching out' and 'potting on'. She rehoused them in three elegant and slender terracotta pots, and then proceeded to slice their tops off with her garden knife. It was as much as I could do to resist jumping in the car and driving the 180 miles home to do likewise to my remaining plants. She seemed so insistent that it was done straight away, that I was afraid they would all be dead by the time we got back home.

As it was, they weren't, and as it is, they would have been better off if I hadn't come back at all. Immediately after we returned, I clicked the scissors from the body of my Swiss Army knife and proceeded to snip. Fifteen times. I did this in accordance with gardening principle number one (not only had I read that this was standard practice, but Mum had also concurred). Principle number two, I realize now, is in need of amendment. Stuff does indeed, generally, grow – but an additional proviso should read 'but only if you don't cut off its really important bits'. What I have done fifteen times, and Mum thrice, is something called 'stopping'. Considering the fact that we have done this before the poor things had a chance to flower, I fear that in this case this word may well turn out to be more accurate, literal and terminal than perhaps it is intended to be.

It now looks highly likely that these tomatoes will bear no fruit whatsoever, and all I will have gained through growing them will be a little more oxygen and a pleasant smell in the bedroom (a novelty in itself), which is more than I would have had if I'd not bothered trying. And if they all fall over tomorrow, I can say that I have learned three important things:

1 Your mother is not always right.
2 Stuff does 'just grow', but some stuff is more resistant to attempts to make it do otherwise than others.
3 If something comes in a packet with instructions written on the back, then it is as well to follow them in the manner in which they were written – precisely.

I'm off to pot them on anyway, because they may, by some fluke, produce something later in the summer – if I don't give them a chance to stretch their legs, then I am effectively reducing that already slim possibility to zero. Besides, it gives me an opportunity to run my hands through some potting compost which is, to me at least, a far more pleasant experience than eating a tomato.

1 May

As well as putting fifteen decapitated tomato plants in lovely, capacious new pots full of fresh, moist compost *just in case* I haven't killed them already, Steve and I accidentally planted ninety-six potatoes yesterday. Not in the sense that we spent a couple of hours at the plot, after which we looked in turn at each other and the potato bed as if to say, 'Well bugger me, what's gone and happened there, then?' It was more that we had indeed intended to plant our maincrop potatoes yesterday afternoon, but did not expect to get all of them in.

I suppose that, once we had performed some distracting but necessary allotment maintenance chores, we got into a planting rhythm, dancing around each other with ease and fluidity, certainly compared to the stiff and clumsy ritual of our first sowing just over a month ago. I was, of course, delighted (and probably more than a little smug and self-satisfied) to note – audibly and repeatedly – how well these forty-four Maris Pipers and fifty-two Pink Fir Apples fitted into the space which remained in the bed. There was an empty half-row after we had finished, but I blame Steve for that, as he'd obviously planted his share a little too close together. It was that, or when I was doing the calculations I forgot to take into account the fact that netting bags vary in size, as does my fist depending on how tightly it is clenched. Another valuable lesson learned for next year.

These tubers are now sitting pretty, at the correct depth and in seven pinstripe-straight rows which are earthed up sufficiently to prevent bomb damage. I for one am not going to be out-ridged by anyone, not even by the guy from the plot to the west of ours who, as it turns out, is not a miserable old sod at all, as I once suspected, but, a bit like me, is just a little shy and prefers to keep his own counsel and company. We nod, smile and say 'Hi' to each other now. Still no idea what his name is, nor he mine I should imagine, but that doesn't seem to matter.

I think that the other reason why we managed to get all the potatoes in yesterday is because everything I have read suggests that maincrops have to be in by the end of April, so we therefore logically assumed that not only all potatoes planted on or after the first of May would fail horribly, but that this would somehow cause everything else to shrivel up and die as well. This may sound idiotic (as indeed it is), but we are still finding our way, and would hate to do anything through complacency to make tomato truncation seem a positively sensible and horticulturally viable course of action.

About now is the anniversary of Steve and I first discussing the possibility, point and absurdity of having our own allotment. Perhaps, then, it would be appropriate to pause to consider where we are, and how far we have come. In terms of the allotment itself, we have six agriculturally viable beds, all squared, weeded and nourished. All but one of these are, to a lesser or greater extent, planted up with something intentional, recognizable and labelled. Most of what we have planted seems to be growing well, as far as my novice eyes can see, and certainly no worse than anyone else's. We have built our own shed, complete with functioning window, door, bench and lock and have also managed to fabricate a larger-than-we-really-need compost bin. In the 'garden' I have six healthy-looking raspberry canes interplanted with some similarly robust-looking garlic, along with various herbs and a small bay tree (almost certainly a shrub, but I still don't know the difference). The leeks have begun to point greenly skywards in their miniature bed, and could well be ready to be thinned for salads or soups in the next month or so before we plant them out. The greenhouse is looking a little sorry for itself due to lack of funds, but still provides just enough shelter for the fifty-odd cos lettuces donated to Steve by a work colleague, along with the headless, hapless tomatoes.

7 May

I spent a blissful and hot couple of hours on Sunday morning pricking out some rocket seedlings which have been coming on nicely and secretively on the kitchen window sill. I stashed them 'inside' the greenhouse. I use inverted commas in a similar manner to those which habitually surround my 'garden': the interior of the greenhouse is still only nominally so due to the fact that Steve and I have resigned ourselves to neglecting it until the autumn. We cannot seem to find the time, money or inclination to sort it out now. Therefore, our greenhouse is currently a construction which keeps everything inside much drier, but not an awful lot warmer, than the outside, which leads me to believe that we may as well have put the pointy bits at the bottom. Those lettuces and 'tomatoes' do look awfully thirsty.

I also transplanted some chives and Welsh onions which Mum had donated, from their temporary patch of soil to three old wheels which I removed from a car before leaving it at the council vehicle dump. Had I not done so, I would have been charged fifteen pounds to pay for their recycling. Having been dragged up proper, I had never before attempted to take all four wheels off a car, and certainly never in freezing-cold February rain while being watched by three oily, smirking geezers who had done it hundreds of times. A word of advice – if you don't want to feel like Penelope Pitstop in *Wacky Races* when one of these guys comes to your rescue with a fork-lift truck, take three fivers with you as well as the bus fare home. However, the wheels had everything going for them in terms of growing stuff – they would hold soil and provide drainage. I also thought that they looked kind of interesting, so along with the alliums, I popped in some Tall Scotch Prize marigold seeds which I had brought back from Heligan, and some Tom Thumb nasturtiums which Mum had sent down for the boys.

After this, I put some sweet peas in terracotta pots (assorted sizes, from the tip, about three dozen for a fiver) and placed the whole lot inside an upturned postcard display rack, two of which – one large, one small – I removed from a skip in Winchester last year. The small one now serves very well, with the addition of some green plastic sheeting, as a lampshade in my sitting room, suspended at just the right height for Steve to crack his head on and swear lividly at every time he gets up. The large one, I felt, would be an interesting alternative to a trellis or canes for the sweet peas to climb. I knew that it would serve this purpose well, as I had seen the bindweed do just that last year while the rack was sitting around waiting for me to come up with a use for it.

Later on, I wandered up to the plot with Charlie, who proved invaluable when it came to standing in the sunniest spot he could find and looking confused, while I busied myself with both types of hoe, weeding with one, followed by drawing flat-bottomed drills for the last of the peas with the other. It turned out that we did not have quite enough peas to fill all the designated areas, but fortunately Ted has very kindly donated not only a dozen or so runner bean seeds but also some bamboo canes for them to grow up and some stout wire to tie them together with. Neither Steve nor I is particularly fond of runner beans, but as with the tomatoes (along with, to be honest, most vegetables) this is hardly the point – we don't like couch grass and mare's tail much either, but we seem to be doing a marvellous job of growing a bumper crop of both.

On Wednesday, Steve and I forged ahead with all the jobs we should have done previously. I started proceedings by dragging him into the shed and kicking his shins until he made sufficiently appreciative noises about the shelf I had constructed in there. Only then did I allow him to get on with digging and weeding (again) bed 'd', into which we later deposited the twenty-eight dehydrated yellow husks, like old men's teeth, that are to become our tall, majestic ears of F1 Sundance sweetcorn. While Stevie dug, I creaked our hazardous wheelbarrow to the other side of the park to fetch more pea sticks, which I sunk into the soil next to the prolific and rapidly emerging shoots. We also sowed a row of nasturtiums next to the sweetcorn – good companion flowers, apparently, as well as an attractive and tasty addition to a salad. We emptied the last of our carrot seeds into a drill near the bottom of bed 'b', and did the same with the remnants of my packet of marigolds to fill that bed up.

After this, Daddy duty beckoned for me, so Steve assumed his post as sofa sentry while I gathered my brace of boys and took them for an organic, whole-earth dinner at Pizza Hut using money the provenance of which I am still unsure about, but I have a feeling it was the twenty quid my sister paid into my bank account recently for no apparent reason.

I dropped them back at their mother's house, and met Steve at the plot again. Bed 'e' was in serious need of some attention, as it is getting close to swede sowing time. Steve had brought a couple of tins of beer with him, so we perched the cans atop the uprights of the compost bin, drank moderately, laughed immoderately and dug until we could no longer see what we were doing.

15 May

The allotment seems to be ticking over – a bit of digging where we have yet to plant, a little sowing where we have just dug, a lot of weeding where we have just sown. I feel a little saddened at how rapidly the novelty of seeing things germinate and grow does not exactly wear off, but surely mellows – like the 'Oooohs' and 'Aaaahs' of Guy Fawkes' night which become a shade less heartfelt and convincing for every firework that spins, howls or bangs. What continues to enthral me, however, is not just the fact that stuff 'kind of, well, grows' but just how quickly some of it does so. Even the stuff that we actually wanted to flourish.

A tour round the beds: bed 'a' contains three, or thereabouts, rows each of Foremost, Wilja, Maris Piper and Pink Fir Apple potatoes. First and second earlies appear to be growing on time-lapse, so keen are they to unfurl. The maincrops seem more reticent, but they were planted later, and we are hoping to still be digging them in October, so I'm not concerned about that right now. Bed 'b' plays host predominantly to carrots and onions, the former sown in succession in order to give a staggered harvest. The earlier sowings seem healthy enough on top at least, and the first rows will probably need thinning soon. The onion sets are swelling quietly and satisfyingly halfway in, halfway out of the soil, and even a couple of the ones I grew from seed have made it to bulbousness. The boys' bed 'c' is marching on, with its pot-pourri of peas, garlic, carrots and sweetcorn, and its neighbour, bed 'd', is fully planted with successive peas, block-sown (it pollenates better that way) sweet-corn, a row of nasturtiums and, after yesterday evening's efforts, twelve runner bean seeds sown in a circle, complete with a corresponding number of canes, driven into the ground perpendicularly as opposed to having them form an elongated teepee – apparently they are more prolific this way and are easier to pick. Moving south to bed 'e', we find absolutely nothing of any interest because this is where we are shortly going to sprinkle the tiny swede seeds. Just above this, bed 'f' currently supports a row of peas along each edge, leaving a square in the centre for more sweetcorn which, along with the swedes, we have vowed to get in the next time we are up there. The plot is as good as fully planted up with the crops we planned would be there. All we need now is to keep the weeds down, then sit back and watch it all unfurl, as it should.

25 Relying on Them

First First Earlies

12 June

It may well be, as I mentioned in the previous chapter, that the novelty of dropping seeds into the soil, bidding them farewell and watching them pop back up again has worn off to an extent. And even the satifaction – nay, surprise – of seeing our crops actually growing has become, if not routine, then at least more commonplace than we thought it might. This last point, though, should come with the proviso that I can only so far speak for the leafy, top halves of the root crops; for all I know the bits that count may well have shrivelled and/or already been eaten by something else. Still, the leaves look healthy enough, and I seem to have learned sufficient patience to not dig everything up just to check that we are going to be able to eat this summer.

To that end, in fact, I was about to thin the carrots a couple of weeks ago, but Ted told me not to bother. Apparently, they kind of 'self select', and the potential risk of bruised foliage – the scent of which will have carrot root flies swarming around the crops like oldies piling in to a bring and buy table – is not worth any marginal increase in yield. Advice given by someone who has always known more about a subject than I ever will is something worth taking to heart, especially if it means more time to sit on my backside in front of the shed complaining to Steve about how many things there are to do at the plot, and asking him why he isn't doing them.

Today, though, we decided that we would find out for sure whether the last eight months or so have been the most worthwhile two-thirds of a year of either of our lives, or whether we may as well have spent the time kicking clods of earth and sucking our teeth in a manly but utterly pointless manner. Today, we were going to dig up some potatoes. We arrived at the plot in the afternoon, and we were greeted – after a morning of indifference on the weather's part – by some warm, caressing sunshine as if being finally embraced in the arms of a once coy mistress. Put another way, the weather was kind and ideal for a nice cup of tea and a biscuit before we got started. Which is exactly what we had. As we creaked and stretched our tubular aluminium and striped canvas picnic chairs (from the tip, surprisingly enough, three quid the pair) into accommodating shapes and slopped hot tea into the lid of the flask, we muttered about the weather (Steve reckoned it felt as if he was being embraced in the arms of a once coy mistress), how much beer each of us had in our fridge (Steve one can, me two) and how remarkable it was that the shed was still standing (truly, it is, despite what Ken said). In fact, we chuntered on about anything and everything except how absolutely and disproportionately terrified we both were about the excruciating and seemingly inevitable feelings of failure we were about to endure. If sowing seeds represented a point at which it was possible for us to get it wrong, then we seemed to have arrived at one which would make it horribly patent just how badly wrong that was. I am not in the least bit superstitious, but somehow the success or otherwise of the allotment has come to represent that of everything else in my life. If, as I found it immensely difficult to believe as I swilled the last of the first tea around the bottom of the cup, we had succeeded in growing something edible, I reasoned that so many more things (material *and* important) that had at one point seemed unfeasible may also come to fruition. More bluntly, if we'd buggered up the spuds, not only were we spitting on Mrs Pottinger's grave, but also ruining our chances of doing anything remotely worthwhile with any area of the rest of our lives. That sort of thing doesn't half make your tea taste funny. Or maybe the flask is due for a bit of bicarb.

Eventually, though, we did pick up the courage. To talk to each other about how we felt, that is. We agreed that the imminent possibility of achieving something which had once appeared unattainable was the precise reason we did not wish to find out whether or not we had. Surely it would be better to leave the whole thing as a 'maybe' – then at least the chance that we had succeeded would remain with us forever. If we knew for sure that we had ballsed it all up, then we would have to chalk up yet another Thing Which We'd Got Wrong.

We had nothing to lose, then, really. The dregs of the second cup of tea had ritually hit the dirt, and I offered the marital fork to Steve.

'Do I have to?'

'Well one of us does. Besides, it's about time you did *something* up here.' I sat back down and poured myself another brew. This looked as if it might take a while. Steve hadn't operated a fork for months, and frankly looked rustier than it did. He shuffled round to the south-east corner of the plot where I had, less than three months ago, first interred our first first early.

Ask me what my ex-wife was wearing when she told me that her waters had broken just before Gabriel was born and I would not have the first idea. Probably because it was five o'clock in the morning and at that time of the day it's all I can do to find my own clothes, let alone specify someone else's. It is perhaps worthy of note, then, that I can recall Steve's attire as he plunged his fork into the soil in order to act as midwife to dinner. It is true that Gabe was born nine and a half years ago, and we were digging spuds only half a day ago, but at three this afternoon I was more intent on making sure that Steve was remembering to hold the right end of the fork, and besides, he'd got changed before I saw him this evening in an attempt to confuse me. But, as clear as a June cuckoo, I can still see him in his 'ethnic' print cotton trousers, which most people stopped wearing in the late nineties, his 'Bjork' T-shirt, the eponymous heroine of which was at her best in the late eighties, and pair of sandals which even the late seventies would rather not acknowledge. Fitting, then, that Steve looks remarkably like a man in his late sixties. And yes, I know – sandals. More specifically sandals in conjunction with the pointy end of a fork – little pinky fir apples, perhaps.

Today, though, Steve was dealing with the inaugural 'foremost' haulm, hoping to deliver a dozen or so of its offspring, and thankfully ended the day with all his toes intact and pointing roughly in the right direction. All eleven of them. Before he took that first plunge, he glanced towards me as he made a few wiggles with fork and hips as a golfer addresses a ball with his driver. I supped tea and held up a placard with the words 'QUIET PLEASE' written on it. Ted, Ron, Joyce and the quiet man to the west all respectfully adjusted their caps and leant on their forks as Steve sliced and levered the soil with his. The dense green and lightly, whitely flowered foliage leant away from the fulcrum of the fork's tines, while what we saw emerging from beneath the soil held us transfixed.

There are certain, unrepeatable moments throughout everyone's life – both good and bad – which will never be forgotten. Occasions so rare, memorable or both that they will remain as indelibly imprinted on the retina of the mind's eye as the whorls on the tips of our fingers.

Those moments which bring joy abide because they are like the small pinpricks that are the stars in the blackness of night – highlights to be savoured, wished upon and believed in. Those times which are more harrowing in their permanence persist as reminders to not be so naive, clumsy, rash or plain foolish again. What popped up from the soil earlier on today was all we had wished for, what we did not fully believe would happen, but was certainly savoured with a nice piece of baked trout a couple of hours ago.

Stevie unearthed fourteen off-white and surprisingly clean tubers, all still umbilically tethered to their parent as if frightened of release. As he shook the haulm to rid the plant of soil, a couple fell to the ground with an earthy 'thud'. As I winced, I had to remind myself that these entities were vegetable, not animal. So precious and laden with agendas, meaning and portent had they become over the last few months that their nurture had begun to feel more like parenting than husbandry.

Next it was my turn. After photographing our first-born from as many different angles as there were tubers, I approached the next plant down and, being cautious not to dig too close to it for fear of skewering the edible bits, did likewise. Out popped another dozen smooth, off-white fruits of our eight-month labour. Similar to the first, so little soil clung to them that they were virtually ready for the pot as they were. I was faintly surprised that they were not also conveniently bagged up and date-stamped, ready for us to carry home.

The fact that we walked back with twenty-six potatoes was, to and for us, little short of extraordinary. That two clueless blokes could, in the space of less than a year, achieve a thirteen-fold increase in potato ownership (as well as building their own shed) was, to our previous supermarket mentalities, remarkable. And that we strode away from the plot earlier with a similar exponential rise in our self-worth, self-confidence, and self-knowledge was, although we had not recognized this at the outset, what had defined and shaped our entire reason for being there in the first place. We have achieved something which had, until today, been a rare feat for us both: we have done what we had set out to do. What's more, on this preliminary evidence, we seem to have done it pretty bloody well.

26 Grounded

Mightier Than the Fork

20 September

Neither Steve nor I was in a particularly pleasant place when we took this project on, and we both feel that the allotment has been, in no small way, the salvation of us. Just over a year before we started to dig the plot – every pun intended – I was a couple of weeks into a new teaching job. Having left my previous two employments, under somewhat acrimonious circumstances, I was preparing to introduce a bunch of disaffected East End kids to the joys of three-dimensional design. However, having already suffered a breakdown of sorts three years previously, I had finally learned to spot the signs of impending mental disquiet.

One of these is a leaden, nauseous stomach knotted with loathing and dread, and, on the morning I woke up to face my students for the first time, mine told me something I had suspected throughout my brief teaching career – that to be a good educator you have to care passionately about both your subject and the fate of your charges. That morning, as I called in sick with a 'stomach bug', I had no clue whatsoever, outside of my family and friends, exactly what it was I did care about.

Twelve months and ten days later saw me embark on a venture which has possibly – with the exception of parenthood – given me more cause to care, and has educated me more, than any other.

For his part, Steve had reached a point in his career where he was unsure of where to go next. Promotion in the mental health care industry meant similar horrors to elsewhere: more responsibility, more meetings and more paperwork. Not a wildly irresponsible man, but not one enamoured of bureaucracy either, Steve could see no way of escaping the situation he was in. However, he knew that to stay where he was would only lead to a defection from 'carer' to that most tactful of tropes in his profession – 'client'. It was driving him bonkers.

Thankfully, we did not have to dig for victory but, through becoming part of a system which has gently, and at times surreptitiously, exerted a similar level of control over us as we have over it, we have sifted from the clods (along with the weeds and rocks) enough fragments of sanity to make our lives at worst tolerable and, often now, enjoyable.

The hottest English summer since records began was also the season during which I first felt truly humbled by the staggering beauty, astonishing complexity and blinding simplicity of nature. The end of this summer also marks the end of our first allotment year.

When Steve and I first decided what to grow (based on which vegetables we could eat without gagging) we decided on seven different crops – potatoes, peas, sweetcorn, onions, carrots, leeks and swedes. For a time, I considered withholding any and all information concerning the success or otherwise of our allotment endeavours. I reasoned that this would, perhaps, finally underline that it is the nature and primacy of process which has been fundamental to our enjoyment of the plot rather than the end result. However, I have come to realize that this is not, in fact, strictly true. Just because we find eating vegetables a bit of a worthy chore, it does not necessarily follow that we wished to see all of our crops wilt. It may well be that it is better to have tried to do something and failed than to have tried to do nothing and succeeded, but given the choice, I would much rather have tried to do something, and succeeded.

Which is, on and in our own terms, exactly what we did. Our allotment has produced more than one type of harvest, but I feel it would be appropriate to detail what worked, practically speaking, and what was, euphemistically, more of a learning experience.

One last trip round the beds, then. Bed 'a', which was full of potatoes really did turn out to be very full of potatoes. As documented in the previous chapter, we dug the first of our first earlies in early June, and ate them while they were still wriggling, lathered in an obscene amount of unsalted butter and dotted with the tangy green Os of roughly chopped chives and Welsh onions from the garden (where now, above the lawn which finally stripped it of its inverted commas, the glorious trumpets of a convolvulus cneorum follow the sun like small purple satellite dishes tracking a signal).

We have stored the majority of our Pink Fir Apples and Maris Pipers (the last of which we dug up only recently) in a large cardboard box stuffed with newspaper in a corner of Steve's garage. It was either this, or make a clamp, as detailed in *The Vegetable Garden Displayed*. This looked like an extremely satisfying thing to construct, but even reading about doing so made me feel somewhat fatigued and dizzy. First, you need to dig a large oblong hole about a foot deep in the ground, then line it with straw. The size of this hole naturally depends on the quantity of potatoes, and this book was obviously published in the days when people could still be trusted to use a little common sense, as no dimensions are given. After this, your potatoes need to be arranged, according to the photograph, in a formation roughly resembling an elongated pyramid. I think theirs must have been glued in place, so regular is their placement. These should then be covered with more generous quantities of straw, to 'allow for a period of sweating'. Not only do potatoes have a right way up, but they also sweat. I'm getting to like them more and more. Finally, the clamp is finished by heaving a good quantity of soil onto the resulting pile and bashing it flat into a shape which could well be a creditable and quite skilled attempt at an architectural model of a thatched barn roof surrounded by a moat.

Apparently, as well as allowing them to sweat, a clamp performs the role of a light-free, cool – but frost-free – storage area for overwintering potatoes. So does a large cardboard box stuffed with newspaper in a corner of Steve's garage, and arranging that didn't expend more energy than the potatoes contain. There should be enough in there to keep the three of us going over the winter, and halfway into spring next year. Perhaps the last of them (barring some of the inevitably left-over sprouting tubers which we will save and replant) will become, along with some onions, a good, thick soup, maybe with the addition of some leeks, which seem to be doing fine having followed the first early potatoes into some slim, watery holes in the soil.

The onion and carrot bed (b) became something of an obsession for me. The interplanting of the two seemed to work well, as did the assiduous observance of the suggestion that carrots should only be weeded on overcast days or after sunset, as these are the times when the root fly becomes inactive. Not all the carrots were exactly 'laang, straight and reliable' but nor were many of them the short, fat and untrustworthy roots we were expecting. In fact I have a suspicion that there were a few envious mutterings from our allotment neighbours when they saw what we managed to pull out – plenty of them were indeed almost pornographically long and straight, and a few really did look like something which Bugs Bunny would have crunched on quite happily. One evening, just as I was pulling up some really quite obscenely long, thick and single-rooted carrots, Dick ambled past. He looked down and, admiring the sturdiness of the Autumn Kings, congratulated me on this success, his teeth glued together in a smile as forced as rhubarb. This led me to suspect that he might be regretting that I'd remembered the good advice he'd given me a few months previously.

The onion sets obliged handsomely, and again should keep us from that section of Tesco's well into next year. They didn't grow to huge proportions, but just so much as looking at the red ones was enough to get the tears welling – raw in a salad they could have felled an elephant but fried, with a little pepper, salt, garlic and whatever meagre amount of butter was left after the potatoes, until they were sticky and caramelized made even the cheapest barbecued burger taste as if it might at some point have been driven past a cow. I kept that bed immaculate this summer – naturally Steve, who actively enjoys weeding, was invaluable as always, but I took it upon myself to ensure that as soon as anything unsolicited dared raise its head, I would pull it out, break it in half and wave the two pieces at the rest of the bed as a warning. Of the original seventy seeds, only two of my hand-reared onions pulled through – both of them reds. I stopped short (just) of naming them, but I would like to say that, in terms of taste, texture and flavour they were worth every minute of the time I lavished on them. I would *love* to say that, but it would be utter balls. They tasted like onions. This was not, however, particularly important – what mattered to me most of all was the fact that I had overseen their development from one type of pot to another, and one of the greatest pleasures for me recently was when I put their tops and tails in the compost. Partly this was because it represented an holistic and poetic activity, closing and opening as it did the loops of two life cycles, but mainly it gave me immense joy because it meant that I had just chopped the ungrateful little bastards' heads off.

The boys' plot was also a success – between them they harvested carrots, peas, garlic and sweetcorn, the first two of which I could not stop them eating straight from the ground and pod respectively. This is a great deal more rewarding than making a rope swing which doesn't swing, as is watching their faces react to the admiring noises made by my family when eating their bursting sweetcorn while on holiday this year. I realized then that I could have banged on about gardening, life cycles and all manner of things which meant nothing to them until I was hoarse, but my children are smart enough to be sceptical about theories until they can taste the results.

Bed 'd' provided more runner beans than we knew

what to do with, which to our minds equates to any-thing more than three, but in actuality meant three every time we turned our backs. I had heard vague mention that, at some point in the past, someone had attempted to use them as a foodstuff, which naturally intrigued me no end. I found that this was indeed possible, providing that they are boiled for around three days and served with a pint of vodka. In this bed we also grew more sweetcorn and peas, the former orig-inally grown after outright insistence from Steve, who proceeded to forget to eat any throughout the summer.

By the time we sowed the swedes, our technique involved a sturdy boot for both drawing and covering the drill and scattering the seeds as accurately as we would have fed them to chickens. Considering the amount of food we got from them, we would have been better off doing just that. We also omitted to either weed between them or thin them out, our sole excuse for which was that we were, by this point, bored of doing so. In spite of this, bed 'e' did indeed provide us with, if not 1,800 of them (I think ten might be pushing it), then certainly at least one swede which did indeed weigh more than our entire initial seed collection and its constrictive elastic band.

In bed 'f' we again had plenty more peas and sweet-corn, proving to me that the benefits of companion planting can't be overstated, the peas around the outside and the corn in a block in the middle.

In purely practical terms, then, we felt that we could confidently call our inaugural year an outright and resounding success, notwithstanding some hiccoughs along the way. I had been right about being wrong about the tomatoes, which met a blind, arid and somewhat ignominious end alongside the cos lettuces and a score and a half of leafy, peppery rocket plants. But all this was happening in the garden, which only ever really served as a distraction from the main event – a sub-plot.

Overall, though, we have achieved more than we had realistically hoped for. The success of the harvest in the traditional sense of the word, although important to Steve and me in terms of our self-respect and male pride, is by no means the only way in which the allotment has benefited and sustained both of us. Neither Steve nor I had a particularly strong history of seeing projects through to their conclusion before we started digging. Therefore, the fact that we took a weed-infested and trash-laden patch of land, made it fertile and fed ourselves off it perhaps means more to us than it would to some others. Our plot has consequently enabled both of us to be more persistent in our respective careers, and to take more control of our lives. I'm glad I thought of it now.

Appendix I: Veg Fact Sheets

Crop: CARROTS

Varieties: St Valery, Autumn King II

Preferred Soil and Position

Sow in warm, moist soil which is free of large stones and has been broken to a fine tilth just prior to sowing. Do not sow in over-rich soil. Prefer a sunny aspect, and a very slightly acid soil (pH 4.5–6.5).

Sowing and Planting Out

Sow thinly in finely raked soil half an inch deep in rows 12" apart. Sow in succession between March and July. Before sowing, apply 120 g per square metre of fish meal or ash to provide the necessary potassium.

Companions / Parasites / Pests / Remedies

Main enemy is the root fly. Avoid bruising the leaves at all times as it is their scent which attracts the fly. Best buddies are leeks, onions and garlic, but they'll also get along famously with beans, lettuce, turnips and parsnips. They don't like dill much, though. Further protection can be given in the form of a home-made garlic spray (see *Notes*, below).

Harvesting and Storing

Pull from August to October. Store in an outbuilding in boxes of sand. Can also be stored in a clamp (see p. 303), but making one of these for carrots doesn't look any easier than doing so for potatoes, so cardboard boxes and newspaper it is.

Notes

- One source suggests crumbled mothballs mixed in with the soil to deter root fly, but God alone knows what this makes your carrots taste like. It doesn't specify how many balls per square metre, but does go on to suggest that a length of string dipped in creosote and laid next to the row will rid the entire plot of pretty much anything with a sense of smell.
- Thin seedlings on dull days or after sunset to minimize root-fly attack. Also, firm the rows after thinning.
- Yield per 30 ft row is approximately 25 lb.
- In a scheme of rotation, they should be grown after brassicas.
- Cylindrical varieties (e.g. Autumn King) can be sown and grown under cloches in August for cropping in November or December.
- The foliage is edible and rich in vitamin K.
- Apply a heavy mulch to promote better root growth.
- Grow some chives nearby. Make that garlic chives – the smell deters the root fly.
- If thinning the carrots, break off some of the stalks and sprinkle them over Ken's plot, which will distract the fly.
- When finished, crush and roughly tear the chives into the buttery pan of freshly dug new potatoes you are going to eat with some sweet baby carrots.
- To make garlic spray, soak about 100 g of chopped garlic bulbs in a few teaspoons of mineral oil for 24 hours. Then add a pint of water in which 10 g of soft soap has been dissolved. Stir and store strained liquid in a non-metallic container. Don't for God's sake use it neat, but dilute it 1:20 in water. Gets rid of most stuff as well as DDT and doesn't give you cancer.

Crop: SWEETCORN

Varieties: F1 Indian Summer, F1 Sundance

Preferred Soil and Position

Aspect is more important than soil type. Try to protect from wind, and stake mature plants if exposed. Prefer plenty of sun. Fertilize soil before planting at a rate of 2 oz per square yard. If bringing on seedlings in a propagator, harden off before planting out.

Sowing and Planting Out

Sow in a propagator mid-April to late May, and plant out mid-May to late June (mid-June for Sundance). Sow in decent compost, cover with about an inch. Plant out with 15″ between each plant, in a block as opposed to in rows – this will help them to pollenate more efficiently. For similar reasons, sow different varieties in separate locations.

Companions / Parasites / Pests / Remedies

Early potatoes, luckily enough, are good companions, so it would seem to make sense to pop a seedling into each space left by a dug-up spud. Other happy companions are peas, beans, dill, cucumbers and squashes. So is bindweed due to its root secretions, but considering we've spent the last 4 months trying to dig the bloody stuff out, I'm going to ignore that.

Harvesting and Storing

Cobs are ready when their tassels have turned dark brown – between the beginning of August and the end of September (mid-September for Sundance). To check for ripeness, squeeze a grain or two – liquid will come out. If it's watery, it's not ripe; creamy is just right; and doughy and thick means you should have been here yesterday.

Notes

· When weeding, don't hoe too close to the plants themselves – they have shallow root systems which could be damaged.

· Roots can appear at the base of the stem. As they do, earth them up or mulch them. Do not remove side shoots, but it's possible that the removal of basal shoots can increase yield.

· In areas with really hungry and/or persistent birds, netting may be necessary.

· Worm cultures are particularly good for sweetcorn. I might have dreamed this, but surely they're not going to do any harm.

Crop: LEEKS

Varieties: Firena, Autumn Giant 3

Preferred Soil and Position

Will grow in most soils, but preferably well prepared – dug and manured or composted. Prefer a pH neutral soil – 6.5–7.

Sowing and Planting Out

Sow in a finely raked seedbed half an inch deep in rows which are 9–12″ apart, in March or April. Transplant in June/July by making a hole 4–6″ deep, dropping in the plants and filling the hole with water. Allow 15″ between rows. Christopher Lloyd recommends planting them in trenches, as this makes for easier earthing up (blanching) later in the season.

Companions / Parasites / Pests / Remedies

Companions – beans, peas, carrots, turnips. From what I can gather, they seem to be pretty much disease/pest-free. Carrots seem to be top companion – alliums generally deter carrot root fly, and carrots are effective at warding off the onion fly and leek moth.

Harvesting and Storing

Use thinnings for soups and salads. Harvest both varieties from mid-September onwards. Both will overwinter and Autumn Giants will crop until early May the following year.

Notes

· Plant out in same soil as early potatoes, having first dug in a decent amount of good well-rotted manure and chicken manure.
· Yield for a 30 ft row is approximately 30 lb.
· Water the seedbed, if dry, the day before planting. Leeks need water. Ha ha.
· To blanch, draw up dry soil, making sure it does not get between the layers of the stems – unless of course you want to spend hours cleaning them, or you like mud in your soup.
· Summer feeding will increase the thickness of the stems.
· If a leak is bolting, lift it and slice it to the centre longitudinally and remove the flower stem – the remainder will still be tender.
· Trim tops and tails before transplanting.

Crop: ONIONS

Varieties: Brunswick, Bedfordshire Champion

Preferred Soil and Position

Finely raked and well-manured soil – light, deep loam ideally. Full sun preferred. Rake in 90 g per square metre of fertilizer before planting. Prefer a slightly acid soil (pH 4.5–6.5).

Sowing and Planting Out

Sow 3–4 seeds to a pot in a propagator at 15–20 degrees C, commencing end of February. Plant out half an inch deep, 2″ apart in rows 12″ apart. Can also be planted out directly later (March onwards) but this sounds risky to me. A second thinning should be made to leave the plants approximately 4″ apart.

Companions / Parasites / Pests / Remedies

Companions – camomile planted a yard or so apart; other than this only carrots are recommended. Avoid planting near beans or cabbages.

Harvesting and Storing

To aid ripening, don't bend the foliage over as some books recommend. The seed packet suggests lifting them carefully and to finish ripening outdoors or in a greenhouse. Store by tying into ropes, or on slatted trays in a dry, airy place. Do not handle in very frosty weather unless using them immediately.

Notes

· Crop rotation especially important to protect against onion eelworm.
· Break off flower stems as and when they appear.
· Approximate yield from a 30 ft row is 22 lb.
· Bracken makes a good mulch and slug deterrent.

Crop: PEAS

Varieties: Onward, Ambassador

Preferred Soil and Position

Like a sunny aspect, in a well-cultivated, pH neutral soil.

Sowing and Planting Out

Sow small batches in succession every fortnight to provide a supply from June to September (mid-October for Onward). Sow from beginning of March to mid-June (Onward) or end of June (Ambassador), 2" deep in 6" wide, flat-bottomed drills. Allow 2 ft between rows and support plants with sticks.

Companions / Parasites / Pests / Remedies

Pests include aphids, bean seed fly, pea moth and pea thrips. Good preventive companions are carrots, beans, sweetcorn and cucumber, although limited attack by pea and bean weevils can be advantageous (see *Notes*).

Harvesting and Storing

Harvest from early June until the end of September (Ambassador) or mid-October (Onward). Best eaten before you get them home, or even leave the plot, but can be frozen, once shelled, if you absolutely have to.

Notes

- Do not sow Ambassador too thickly, as it is a vigorous variety. If peas suffer overcrowding, then the yield will be reduced.
- Some studies have shown that pea yields have actually been increased when the tips of their tendrils have been removed by pea and bean weevils. It is therefore possibly beneficial to do this by hand. I mentioned this to Ted, and he replied by telling me that he has been removing the tendril-tips of his magnificent sweet peas for half a century.
- Protect young plants by using netting or black cotton stretched between 'twiggy' sticks. These sticks also give the plants something to climb up, but they don't like ash, apparently.
- Water regularly during dry spells, and mulch using leaf-mould or garden compost.
- Pick peas regularly. The yield will be reduced if pods are allowed to mature. More importantly, they won't taste anywhere near as good.
- Do not cook fresh peas. It is, or should be, a crime beaten only narrowly in heinousness by freezing them. Strip the pods with the tip of the thumb straight into any decent salad or, even better, straight into your mouth.

Crop: POTATOES

Varieties: Foremost, Wilja, Maris Piper, Pink Fir Apple

Preferred Soil and Position

Open position in full sun – too much shade and the tops will become spindly. Prefer well-dug and manured or composted soil (dig in about a bucketful per square yard). Two weeks before planting, apply fertilizer at about 2–3 oz per square yard.

Sowing and Planting Out

Lay out – or 'chit' – tubers in egg boxes in an airy, light place (but not in full sun) in January. Sprouts should ideally be half to one inch long by planting time, which for first earlies is March to early April, second earlies early to mid-April and maincrops late April. Earlies should be planted in rows which are 18″ apart, with 12″ between each tuber, and mains should be in rows 2 ft apart with 18″ between each tuber.

Companions / Parasites / Pests / Remedies

Main threat is potato blight. Keep well watered and earth up regularly (see *Notes*). Risk of wireworm can be reduced by ensuring thorough digging, especially of newly cultivated land. Beneficial companion plants include marigolds, aubergine, beans, sweetcorn, horseradish, cabbage and foxgloves.

Harvesting and Storing

First earlies can be harvested from early June until mid–end of July, second earlies from July until September, and mains should be left in until September but dug well before first frosts. All potatoes should be stored in a cool, absolutely dark place. One book suggests building an enormous clamp which looks like hard work; luckily, another, obviously more reliable, tome assures me that a large cardboard box stuffed with newspaper will do just as well.

APPENDIX I

Notes

- Earthing Up – as soon as the first shoots appear, they should be covered with a draw hoe. This should be repeated every one to two weeks until the foliage of one row is touching that of the next. This process helps to protect potatoes against potato blight, and the increased ratio of root to haulm also increases the yield of each plant. Some folks grow spuds inside car tyres, adding an extra tyre, and extra soil, as the plants reach upwards. A bit like pouring water over a drowning man, but with more desirable consequences.
- Larger tubers may be cut in half, preferably lengthways, and used as two separate seeds providing that both resultant pieces have healthy sprouts.
- Apparently, potatoes grown under stringently controlled conditions demonstrate a growth rhythm which directly reflects the waxing and waning of the lunar cycle.

Crop: SWEDES

Varieties: Brora, Ruby

Preferred Soil and Position

Prefer an alkaline soil – add lime if necessary. Like well-cultivated soil and an open position, as swedes are traditionally a field-based crop and have grown accustomed to wind and open ground.

Sowing and Planting Out

Sow directly into finely raked, warm and moist soil, half an inch deep in rows approximately 18" apart. Thin seedlings to approximately 8" apart by degrees. Sow Brora from mid-April to mid-June, and Ruby from mid-May to mid-June.

Companions / Parasites / Pests / Remedies

Flea beetle can be prevented by keeping plants well-watered, preferably every evening after sunset. Club root can be prevented by the addition of lime. Make sure that there are no dandelions or docks near to swedes as they attract the cutworm moth.

Harvesting and Storing

Harvest before first frost. Can be stored in sand in a dry shed, although one book suggests that they can, in fact, be left in the ground over the winter to be harvested as and when required.

Notes

· Swedes, along with leeks, Brussels sprouts and a few others, can be left in situ and harvested as and when required.
· A compatible succession crop is the broad bean, planted early the following spring.
· Swedes thrive best in an alkaline soil of around pH 7–8.
· Swedes do not require a great deal of feeding. However, it is best to weed them, thin them and generally remember they are there on a more than quarterly basis.
· The approximate average yield from just under 5 g of swede seeds is, when thinned to 12" apart, a shade over 34 kilos.

Appendix II: Allotted History

The Surprisingly Interesting Bit

Allotments are the diversely textured and richly coloured patches of land often found alongside railway lines,
roads, parks, rivers and canals. They are frequently
shoehorned into spaces which are – geographically or
politically – too awkward or contentious for any other
purpose. Indeed throughout history allotments – and
their sometimes instrumental role in many of our more

pivotal moments in agricultural and industrial history – have been an awkward thorn in many a politician's (not to mention landowner's) side.

To those strolling along a canal bank on a sunny June afternoon and waving to a chap called Alf, who smiles and raises his hand-fork in reply as he thins his carrots, allotment life is somehow as large a part of English Country Life as a game of village cricket or the painted narrowboats whose occupants will also wave benignly and contentedly at any pedestrian onlooker willing to spare the time. I should clarify here that, although I use the word 'English' in this context, pockets of allotments can be found in rural and urban areas throughout the United Kingdom. The political history glanced at here is that of parliamentary acts governing allotments, to varying extents, in England, Wales and Northern Ireland. However, the social and political history of these is mirrored, by and large, by that of land ownership or otherwise north of the border.

Allotments seem to have remained predominantly in locations which can be viewed by curious onlookers as they walk, ride, drive or float by, as if they were part of a large theme park called the 'British Experience'. Visitors to this particular attraction can see all that they need in terms of reassurance that life is as it should be and that everything is okay. They can see comfort, harmony, effective hard work, banter and bonhomie. What they observe is, on the whole, people relaxing, having fun, working because they choose to and keeping fit while growing food they can trust. They see people at leisure, and they see people at peace. They therefore see, chronologically speaking, approximately only five per cent of the otherwise polemic, violent and sometimes bloodthirsty history of allotments in many parts of Britain.

In retrospect, it could be viewed as vaguely ironic that it was not until a few months *after* I suggested that Ken is around 900 years old that I discovered that British allotments can, in one form or another, be traced back to the early twelfth century. This was the period of time when, not content with the amount of power and land already afforded them by the legacy of the arcanely hierarchical system of Norman feudalism, many noblemen began to enclose, and claim as their own, what was previously common land. When the peasants complained that this course of action was not acceptable or, indeed, legal, the landowners simply made it so by virtue of the fact that most of them were also politicians and proceeded to invent and implement a rash of local Inclosure Acts. They would then stick their fingers in their ears and blow raspberries at the riff-raff from the other side of the wall which surrounded what was now *their* land, so there, and they continued in this vein over the next few centuries.

The right which allowed the common man's use of common land, or land designated as 'waste' by those who owned it, for the purposes of gathering food and fuel or for grazing their animals dated back to the Anglo-Saxon period, so it was understandable that many people took great exception to these enclosures – mainly because this course of action dispossessed them of the only way of life they, and any of their relatives, had ever known. They did one or two things – they either migrated to the ever expanding towns and cities to find an alternative way of life, or they starved to death.

Difficult as it may be to believe, Gerrard Winstanley and the Diggers was not a one-hit Yorkshire beat combo from 1964, but were, in fact, a band of fearless renegades who set up an agricultural colony on someone else's land in Surrey in 1649. They did this in protest at these increasingly restrictive Inclosure Acts which were making it more and more difficult for those not born into the aristocracy to feed their families. Of course, the landowner was quick to hound these insurgents from his territory, after first destroying their crops and razing their houses.

The protests escalated, however, and it is these

uproars which gave direct rise, in 1715, to the Riot Act, which any landowner was empowered to read to any angry, incensed and increasingly hungry crowd. He was also permitted to 'cut down' any protagonists who remained after this course of action. The Black Acts of 1723 further consolidated the Riot Act by introducing fifty new 'offences' against the Inclosure Act, punishable by death. From this point on, with the hoi-polloi suitably repressed and with the tightening stranglehold of industrialization being felt by all but the most remote areas of rural Britain, the debate festered and rumbled for over a century.

By the early nineteenth century, considering the appalling working conditions in factories and the short life expectancy of their workers, hundreds of thousands of people had probably realized what a dreadful mistake they had made when they had judged working in a cotton mill to be preferable to slow starvation. Most of the revolting peasants who had not been 'cut down' had opted for at least enough food on the table, even if it meant that they had only three fingers to eat it with. Some, though, still did try to supplement their three-pieces-of-gravel-a-week wage by taking the risk of working small strips of what common land was left. Where there was none, the introduction of the Poor Laws ensured, albeit with strings attached, that provision was made for paupers to earn accommodation and food by working a designated strip of land.

Probably the most important piece of modern legislation in the history of allotments was enacted in 1845 – the General Inclosure Act. What sets this document apart from all other related papers is the inclusion of the mandatory provision of allotments to the 'labouring poor'. Despite the fact that this Act was a little vague on the quality, quantity and accessibility of these plots, as well as how much landlords were allowed to charge for them, this represented a huge step forward for those previously denied their right to work the land and, after male farm workers were allowed the vote for the first time in 1884, this Act was more tightly regulated by the Allotment Acts of 1887 and 1890. Scotland, from what I can ascertain, seemed to manage to get all this stitched up with a single Allotments (Scotland) Act in 1892, which was amended once in 1950.

Devolution of power over allotment issues to local authority level did not take place until 1908, however, and it was not until the Allotment Act of 1922 – a full four years after the First World War ended, and three years after the Land Settlement Act of 1919 which made special provision for returning servicemen – that it was stipulated that allotments should be available to all, not just the 'labouring poor'. Since then, allotment usage soared to a wartime peak of just over one and a half million tended plots.

The most recent report on allotments, carried out by the Office of the Deputy Prime Minister in 1998, reckoned this figure now to be nearer two hundred and fifty thousand. This number is, evidently, continually decreasing. Without wishing to transform this overview to the level of polemic, it is my impression that allotments, although no longer strictly necessary for the provision of food, are one of the few remaining places in an increasingly frenetic society where, if you sit still enough, for long enough, you can just discern the movement of the hour hand on a clock. The same report from the ODPM contains the following quotes:

> *Many of the submissions (of survey questionnaires) we received noted the contribution that allotment gardening can make to physical and mental good health*

and,

> *We recommend that health authorities recognize and exploit the therapeutic potential of allotments for people with mental or physical health problems.*

Considering the decline in the necessity to 'dig for victory' in the latter half of the twentieth century, and knowing the huge range of benefits resulting from allotment ownership – which Steve and I have experienced at first hand – surely the next phase in the development of these fascinating microcosms of society must be some kind of initiative where people from all sectors of the community should be encouraged to dig not for necessity, victory or even plenty, but for therapy.

Appendix III:
Suggested Further Reading

The Cassell's Encyclopaedia of Gardening, Anita Pereire, Ward Lock, 1995. Jacket price was thirty quid, but I got it for a fiver in a Help the Aged charity shop. First port of call for any general enquiry from plant identification to laying a patio.

The Collins Handguide to the Trees of Britain and Northern Europe, John Wilkinson and Alan Mitchell, Collins, 1978. An excellent quick-reference guide which is small enough to pop in a rucksack or large pocket when out with the dogs. Only any good for identification purposes during the summer as far as deciduous trees are concerned as they are only depicted with foliage, but still good enough to double the length of time taken for any given walk. Marie Curie Cancer Care shop, 25p.

Field Guide to the Trees and Shrubs of Britain, Reader's Digest, 1981. A little more comprehensive and authoritative than the above, but still definition deficient when it comes to differentiating between the two eponymous plants. More accurate drawings plus some depictions of deciduous trees in winter. The copy referred to in the main text belongs to Steve, and has enabled him to make a new distinction in tree identification other than 'oak' – there is now 'not oak'. He has no idea where it came from, or how much it cost, which means that he probably nicked it.

Food From Your Garden, various authors, Reader's Digest, 1977. If it's not in here then you probably shouldn't be growing it. Comprehensive guide to 'growing, cooking and preserving your own fruit and vegetables'. 1977? Various authors? Tom and Barbara more like. Also contains some nice little line drawings and colour plates. British Heart Foundation, 40p.

Gardener Cook, Christopher Lloyd, Frances Lincoln, 1997. This is a beautiful book. Its dimensions and weight are just right, it has a lovely waxy cover and some photographs of Christopher's garden nearly as good as mine of our plot. Forthright, dependable and soothing advice. A gift from my gifted sister.

The Gardener's Dictionary of Horticultural Terms, Harold Bagust, Cassell, 1992. I would like to meet Mr Bagust. Most dictionaries need a multiplicity of compilers – not this one; Harold knows his lobate from his pinnate. Fantastic book for those who like to trawl speculatively for gratuitous but sonorous words. A birthday gift from a friend who would rather not be named.

Garden Spells – The Magic of Herbs, Trees and Flowers, Claire Nahmad and Camilla Charnock, Pavilion, 1994. Mostly airy-fairy twaddle, but some interesting stuff about the mythology of flowers in relation to homeopathy and Bach Flower Remedies. Oxfam, £1.50.

The Good Food Growing Guide, John Bond, David and Charles, 1977. If I meet Mr Bagust, can Mr Bond be there too? Quite scientific and exhaustive in its approach, this one. Vast quantities of information laid out in tables and cross-referencing aplenty. Excellent source for companion planting details and a mine of 'well I never' type information. From the tip, 20p.

The Natural Food Catalogue, Vicki Peterson, MacDonald, 1978. I can't pull this one from the bookshelves without immediately being assaulted by the Age of Aquarius and, for some reason, the smell of incense and home-baked brown bread. Contains a good deal of information on how to cook things you did not know were edible (such as runner beans), and a fantastic lentil and pea collage on the cover. Save the Children, 50p.

The New Complete Self-Sufficiency, John Seymour, Dorling Kindersley, 2002. I first bought the original edition of this book in 1991, then foolishly lent it to someone in 1994. I bought my current copy in 2003 from Waterstone's for twenty quid. Worth every penny of the boys' weekly food budget. A fabulous, indispensable book for anyone with the remotest interest in self-sufficient matters; it tells you exactly how you know you want to live your life if only you had the bottle.

Old Wives' Lore for Gardeners, Maureen and Bridget Boland, The Bodley Head, 1977. This is turning out to be some dinner party – Mr Bagust, Mr Bond and the two Madames Boland. A slim volume, but full of 'hocus-pocus' information which has subsequently stood up to scientific rigour. Theories on biodynamic planting (planting according to the phases of the moon), companion planting and welcome advice on deterring cats have all prevailed. British Heart Foundation, 95p.

Organic Gardening, edited by Valerie Duncan, Merehurst, 2000. Reliable, up-to-date, no-nonsense guide to doing things the nice way. Its longer title is *The Gardener's Guide to Organic Gardening*, which always makes me wonder who else it might be aimed at. Some lovely photographs, and a snip at £1.99 (cover price £4.99) from the Heligan bookshop.

Organic Living, Lynda Brown, Dorling Kindersley, 2000. This book is subtitled 'Simple Solutions for a Better Life', and has plenty of quick-reference panels and artsy photographs of lemon squeezers and well-lit close-ups of vegetables in the hands of a 'peasant'. Once past the gloss, though, there is quite a lot of useful information on a range of subjects from organic cotton suppliers to ethical banana farmers. Discount bookshop, £2.99 (from £14.99).

The River Cottage Cookbook, Hugh Fearnley-Whittingstall, HarperCollins, 2001. I don't want Hugh at the dinner party. I want him all to myself. He treats his vegetables the way he treats his animals. With respect and dignity. One of the few recipe writers it is possible to read with no intention of cooking anything. I'd like to have a quiet pint or two with Hugh, but I'm not sure I can afford to be as poor as he is.

Urban Permaculture, David Watkins, Permanent Publications, 1993. A surprisingly readable book, with a good number of realistic and practical suggestions on topics such as the recycling of grey water (washing machine and bath water, for instance) and container gardening. This one came from the tip for 50p.

The Vegetable Garden Displayed, Royal Horticultural Society, 1978. First published in 1941, my copy looks as if it retained the photographs of that edition. A robust guide to all things strictly non-organic, I have no doubt that later editions were more circumspect in their use of really quite unpleasant chemicals. I loved referring to this book mainly because of the black and white photographs of men in pinstriped suits bending over arrow-straight drills, but also because it provided information on growing vegetables as accurate and true as those trenches. From the tip, 20p.